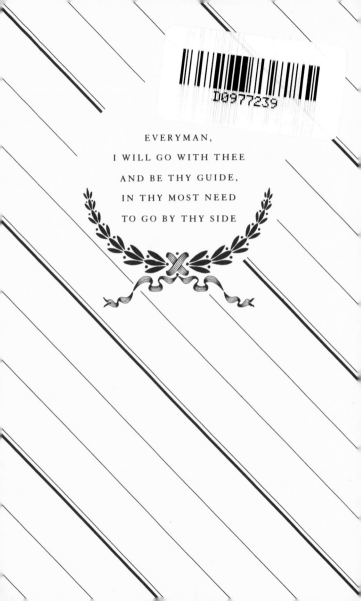

EVERYMAN,
I WILL GO WITH THEE
AND BE THY GUIDE,
IN THY MOST NEED
TO GO BY THY SIDE

EVERYMAN'S LIBRARY
POCKET POETS

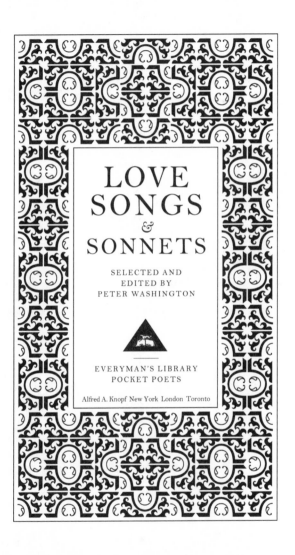

LOVE
SONGS
&
SONNETS

SELECTED AND
EDITED BY
PETER WASHINGTON

EVERYMAN'S LIBRARY
POCKET POETS

Alfred A. Knopf New York London Toronto

THIS IS A BORZOI BOOK
PUBLISHED BY ALFRED A. KNOPF

This selection by Peter Washington first published in
Everyman's Library, 1997
Copyright © 1997 by Everyman's Library
Fourth printing (US)

A list of acknowledgments to copyright owners appears at the back of
this volume.

US website: www.randomhouse.com/everymans

ISBN 0-679-45465-9 (US)
1-85715-731-1 (UK)

A CIP catalogue record for this book is available from the British Library

Typography by Peter B. Willberg

Typeset in the UK by AccComputing, North Barrow, Somerset

Printed and bound in Germany
by GGP Media, Pössneck

CONTENTS

6

9

11

12

13

FOREWORD

This is the fourth and final volume in the Everyman series of love poems. As the title suggests, the emphasis is lyrical: almost every piece in this collection has been set to music or could be, though many are more suited to Weill than to Schubert.

Thematically, I have taken my cue from the first line of the first poem: *Many arrivals make us live.* Variety is the key. Passion, devotion and desire loom large in this collection, but not exclusively. Diverse kinds and conditions of love are celebrated here, for a girl or a place, a pig or a dog; and the tedium of excessive romance is tempered with a sharp draught of suspicion and common sense. Love is said to make the world go round, but overdosing on adorable poems is more likely to make the head spin – or as Swinburne put it:

> A month or twain to live on honeycomb
> Is pleasant; but one tires of scented time,
> Cold sweet recurrence of accepted rhyme,
> And that strong purple under juice and foam
> Where the wine's heart has burst;
> Nor feel the latter kisses like the first.

PETER WASHINGTON

LOVE SONGS
AND SONNETS

THE MANIFESTATION

Many arrivals make us live: the tree becoming
Green, a bird tipping the topmost bough,
A seed pushing itself beyond itself,
The mole making its way through darkest ground,
The worm, intrepid scholar of the soil –
Do these analogies perplex? A sky with clouds,
The motion of the moon, and waves at play,
A sea-wind pausing in a summer tree.

What does what it should do needs nothing more.
The body moves, though slowly, toward desire.
We come to something without knowing why.

THEODORE ROETHKE (1908–1963)

WHOLE LOVE

Every choice is always the wrong choice,
Every vote cast is always cast away –
How can truth hover between alternatives?

Then love me more than dearly, love me wholly,
Love me with no weighing of circumstance,
As I am pledged in honour to love you:

With no weakness, with no speculation
On what might happen should you and I prove less
Than bringers-to-be of our own certainty.
Neither was born by hazard: each foreknew
The extreme possession we are grown into.

INVOCATION

Come out of the dark earth
Here where the minerals
Glow in their stone cells
Deeper than seed or birth.

Come under the strong wave
Here where the tug goes
As the tide turns and flows
Below that architrave.

Come into the pure air
Above all heaviness
Of storm and cloud to this
Light-possessed atmosphere.

Come into, out of, under
The earth, the wave, the air.
Love, touch us everywhere
With primeval candor.

SHALL I COME?

Shall I come, if I swim? wide are the waves, you see:
Shall I come, if I fly, my dear love, to thee?
Streams Venus will appease; Cupid gives me wings;
All the powers assist my desire
Save you alone, that set my woful heart on fire.

You are fair, so was Hero that in Sestos dwelt;
She a priest, yet the heat of love truly felt.
A greater stream than this did her love divide;
But she was his guide with a light:
So through the streams Leander did enjoy her sight.

TO BE IN LOVE

To spring impetuously in air and remain
Treading on air for three heart-beats or four,
Then to descend at leisure; or else to scale
The forward-tilted crag with no hand-holds;
Or, disembodied, to carry roses home
From a Queen's garden – this is being in love,
Graced with *agilitas* and *subtilitas*
At which few famous lovers ever guessed
Though children may foreknow it, deep in dream,
And ghosts may mourn it, haunting their own tombs,
And peacocks cry it, in default of speech.

ROBERT GRAVES (1895–1985)   23

HOME TRAVEL

What need I travel, since I may
More choicer wonders here survey?
What need I Tyre for purple seek,
When I may find it in a cheek?
Or sack the Eastern shores? there lies
More precious diamonds in her eyes.
What need I dig Peru for ore,
When every hair of her yields more?
Or toil for gums in India,
Since she can breathe more rich than they?
Or ransack Africk? there will be
On either hand more ivory.
But look within: all virtues that
Each nation would appropriate,
And with the glory of them rest,
Are in this map at large exprest;
That who would travel here might know
The little world in folio.

AH BED!

Ah bed! the field where joy's peace some do see;
    The field where all my thoughts to war be trained:
How is thy grave by my strange fortune stained!
How thy lee shores by my sighs stormed be!
With sweet soft shades, thou oft invitest me
    To steal some rest; but, wretch! I am constrained –
    Spurred with Love's spur, though gold; and shortly
      reined
With Care's hard hand – to turn and toss in thee!
    While the black horrors of the silent night
    Paint Woe's black face so lively to my sight;
That tedious leisure marks each wrinkled line.
    But when Aurora leads out Phoebus' dance,
    Mine eyes then only wink: for spite, perchance,
That worms should have their sun and I want mine.

SIR PHILIP SIDNEY (1554–1586)

THE AVOWAL

I have lost the wood, the heath,
Fresh Aprils long gone by . . .
Give me your lips: their breath
Shall be the forest's sigh.

I have lost the sullen Sea,
Its glooms, its echoed caves;
Speak only: it shall be
The murmur of the waves.

By royal grief oppressed
I dream of a vanished light . . .
Hold me: in that pale breast
Shall be the calm of night.

TRANS. RICHARD WILBUR

THE LOOK

Strephon kissed me in the spring,
    Robin in the fall,
But Colin only looked at me
    And never kissed at all.

Strephon's kiss was lost in jest,
    Robin's lost in play,
But the kiss in Colin's eyes
    Haunts me night and day.

SARA TEASDALE (1884–1933)   27

DOWN BY THE SALLEY GARDENS

Down by the salley gardens
    my love and I did meet;
She passed the salley gardens
    with little snow-white feet.
She bid me take love easy,
    as the leaves grow on the tree;
But I, being young and foolish,
    with her would not agree.

In a field by the river
    my love and I did stand,
And on my leaning shoulder
    she laid her snow-white hand.
She bid me take life easy,
    as the grass grows on the weirs;
But I was young and foolish,
    and now am full of tears.

CONVICTION (IV)

I like to get off with people,
I like to lie in their arms
I like to be held and lightly kissed,
Safe from all alarms.

I like to laugh and be happy
With a beautiful kiss,
I tell you, in all the world
There is no bliss like this.

STEVIE SMITH (1902–1971)

LOVE DISLIKES NOTHING

Whatsoever thing I see,
Rich or poore although it be;
'Tis a Mistresse unto mee.

Be my Girle, or faire, or browne,
Do's she smile, or do's she frowne:
Still I write a Sweet-heart downe.

Be she rough, or smooth of skin;
When I touch, I then begin
For to let Affection in.

Be she bald, or do's she weare
Locks incurl'd of other haire;
I shall find enchantment there.

Be she whole, or be she rent,
So my fancie be content,
She's to me most excellent.

Be she fat, or be she leane,
Be she sluttish, be she cleane,
I'm a man for ev'ry Sceane.

SYMPHONY RECITAL

I do not like my state of mind;
I'm bitter, querulous, unkind.
I hate my legs, I hate my hands,
I do not yearn for lovelier lands.
I dread the dawn's recurrent light;
I have to go to bed at night.
I snoot at simple, earnest folk.
I cannot take the gentlest joke.
I find no peace in paint or type.
My world is but a lot of tripe.
I'm disillusioned, empty-breasted.
I am not sick, I am not well.
My quondam dreams are shot to hell.
My soul is crushed, my spirit sore;
I do not like me any more.
I cavil, quarrel, grumble, grouse.
I ponder on the narrow house.
I shudder at the thought of men . . .
I'm due to fall in love again.

SECRECY

Lovers are happy
When favoured by chance,
But here is blessedness
Beyond all happiness,

Not to be gainsaid
By any gust of chance,
Harvest of one vine,
Gold from the same mine:

To keep which sacred
Demands a secrecy
That the world might blame
As deceit and shame;

Yet to publish which
Would make a him and her
Out of me and you
That were both untrue.

Let pigeons couple
Brazenly on the bough,
But royal stag and hind
Are of our own mind.

FOUR ARMS, TWO NECKS

Four arms, two necks, one wreathing;
Two pairs of lips, one breathing;
Two hearts that multiply
Sighs interchangeably:

The thought of this confounds me,
And as I speak it wounds me.
It cannot be expressed.
Good help me, whilst I rest.

Bad stomachs have their loathing,
And oh, this all is no thing:
This 'no' with griefs doth prove
Report oft turns to love.

ANON., 1608

I LOOKED OF LATE AND SAW THEE LOOK ASKANCE

I looked of late and saw thee look askance
Upon my door, to see if I sat there,
As who should say: If he be there by chance
Yet may he think I look him everywhere.
No, cruel, no, thou knowest and I can tell
How for thy love I laid my looks aside:
Though thou (percase) hast looked and liked well
Some new-found looks amid this world so wide.
But since thy looks my love have so inchained
That to my looks thy liking now is past,
Look where thou likest, and let thy hands be stained
In true love's blood, which thou shalt lack at last.
    So look, so lack, for in these toys thus tossed,
    My looks thy love, thy looks my life have lost.

DEA EX MACHINA

In brief, shapeliness and smoothness of the flesh are desirable
because they are signs of biological efficiency.
> – David Angus, *The New York Times Book Review*

My love is like Mies van der Rohe's
    'Machine for living'; she,
Divested of her underclothes,
    Suggests efficiency.

Her supple shoulders call to mind
    A set of bevelled gears;
Her lower jaw has been aligned
    To hinge behind her ears.

Her hips, sweet ball-and-socket joints,
    Are padded to perfection;
Each knee, with its patella, points
    In just the right direction.

Her fingertips remind me of
    A digital computer;
She couldn't be, my well-tooled love,
    A millimeter cuter.

JOHN UPDIKE (b. 1932)

SURE PROOF

I can no more describe you
than I can put a thing for the first time
where it already is.

If I could make a ladder of light
or comb the hair of a dream girl with a real comb
or pour a table into a jug . . .

I'm not good at impossible things.
And that is why I'm sure
I will love you for my ever.

THE FINDING OF LOVE

Pale at first, and cold,
Like wizard's lily-bloom
Conjured from the gloom,
Like torch of glow-worm seen
Through grasses shining green
By children half in fright,
Or Christmas candlelight
Flung on the outer snow,
Or tinsel stars that show
Their evening glory
With sheen of fairy story –

Now with his blaze
Love dries the cobweb maze
Dew-sagged upon the corn,
He brings the flowering thorn,
Mayfly and butterfly,
And pigeons in the sky,
Robin and thrush,
And the long bulrush,
Bird-cherry under the leaf,
Earth in a silken dress,
With end to grief,
With joy in steadfastness.

ROBERT GRAVES (1895–1985)   37

TO MISTRESS
MARGARET HUSSEY

Merry Margaret,
    As midsummer flower,
Gentle as falcon
    Or hawk of the tower:
With solace and gladness,
Much mirth and no madness,
All good and no badness;
    So joyously,
    So maidenly,
    So womanly
    Her demeaning
    In every thing,
    Far, far passing
    That I can indite,
    Or suffice to write
Of Merry Margaret
    As midsummer flower,
Gentle as falcon
    Or hawk of the tower
    And patient and still
    And as full of good will
    As fair Isaphill,
    Coliander
    Sweet pomander,

Good Cassander,
   Steadfast of thought,
Well made, well wrought,
   Far may be sought
   Ere that he can find
   So courteous, so kind
As Merry Margaret,
   This midsummer flower
Gentle as falcon
   Or hawk of the tower.

UPON KINDE AND TRUE LOVE

'Tis not how witty, nor how free,
Nor yet how beautifull she be,
But how much kinde and true to me.
Freedome and Wit none can confine,
And Beauty like the Sun doth shine.
But kinde and true are onely mine.

Let others with attention sit,
To listen, and admire her wit,
That is a rock where I'le not split.
Let others dote upon her eyes.
And burn their hearts for sacrifice,
Beauty's a calm where danger lyes.

But Kinde and True have been long tried
A harbour where we may confide,
And safely there at anchor ride.
From change of winds there we are free,
And need not feare Storme's tyrannie,
Nor Pirat, though a Prince he be.

VAIN GRATUITIES

Never was there a man much uglier
In eyes of other women, or more grim:
'The Lord has filled her chalice to the brim,
So let us pray she's a philosopher,'
They said; and there was more they said of her –
Deeming it, after twenty years with him,
No wonder that she kept her figure slim
And always made you think of lavender.

But she, demure as ever, and as fair,
Almost, as they remembered her before
She found him, would have laughed had she been there;
And all they said would have been heard no more
Than foam that washes on an island shore
Where there are none to listen or to care.

E. A. ROBINSON (1869–1935)   41

A FACE THAT SHOULD CONTENT ME WONDEROUS WELL

A face that should content me wonderous well
Should not be fair but lovely to behold,
With gladsome cheer all grief for to expel;
With sober looks so would I that it should
Speak without words such words as none can tell;
Her tress also should be of crisped gold;
With wit: and thus might chance I might be tied,
And knit again the knot that should not slide.

BLEECKER STREET, SUMMER

Summer for prose and lemons, for nakedness and
     langour,
for the eternal idleness of the imagined return,
for rare flutes and bare feet, and the August bedroom
of tangled sheets and the Sunday salt, ah violin!

When I press summer dusks together, it is
a month of street accordions and sprinklers
laying the dust, small shadows running from me.

It is music opening and closing, *Italia mia*, on Bleecker,
ciao, Antonio, and the water-cries of children
tearing the rose-coloured sky in streams of paper;
it is dusk in the nostrils and the smell of water
down littered streets that lead you to no water,
and gathering islands and lemons in the mind.

There is the Hudson, like the sea aflame.
I would undress you in the summer heat,
and laugh and dry your damp flesh if you came.

LOVERS IN WINTER

The posture of the tree
   Shows the prevailing wind;
And ours, long misery
   When you are long unkind.

But forward, look, we lean –
   Not backward as in doubt –
And still with branches green
   Ride our ill weather out.

IF THROUGH THE ICEBOUND MAZES
OF YOUR GRACE

If through the icebound mazes of your grace
   you had vouchsafed a single kiss to guide me,
my heart, though languishing in Polar space,
   might have subdued the winter that defied me.
And had I not the picture of your face
   (that were too much) but of your hair to tide me
over the seas of pain, I'd keep that place
   though angels with the sweets of heaven plied me.
But I have naught of yours in loneliness –
   nor beauty's counterfeit mine eyes to charm,
   nor memory to linger and be warm
within the heart. And though you may profess
   that love is of the spirit, I'll reply:
   how can soul live or love if body die?

PIERRE DE RONSARD (1524–1585)   45
TRANS. HUMBERT WOLFE

THE LOVE SONG

Out of the blackthorn edges
I caught a tune
And before it could vanish, seized
It, wrote it down.

Gave to a girl, so praising
Her eyes, lips and hair
She had little knowing, it was only thorn
Had dreamed of a girl there.

Prettily she thanked me, and never
Guessed any of my deceit...
But O Earth is this the only way
Man may conquer, a girl surrender her sweet?

LOVING TRUE, FLYING BLIND

How often have I said before
That no soft 'if', no 'either-or',
Can keep my obdurate male mind
From loving true and flying blind? –

Which, though deranged beyond all cure
Of temporal reason, knows for sure
That timeless magic first began
When woman bared her soul to man.

Be bird, be blossom, comet, star,
Be paradisal gates ajar,
But still, as woman, bear you must
With who alone endures your trust.

ROBERT GRAVES (1895–1985)   47

CORAL

This coral's shape echoes the hand
It hollowed. Its

Immediate absence is heavy. As pumice,
As your breast in my cupped palm.

Sea-cold, its nipple rasps like sand,
Its pores, like yours, shone with salt sweat.

Bodies in absence displace their weight,
And your smooth body, like none other,

Creates an exact absence like this stone
Set on a table with a whitening rack

Of souvenirs. It dares my hand
To claim what lovers' hands have never known:

The nature of the body of another.

THRICE TOSS THESE OAKEN ASHES IN THE AIR

Thrice toss these oaken ashes in the air,
Thrice sit thou mute in this inchanted chair;
And thrice three times tie up this true loves knot,
And murmur soft, she will, or she will not.

Go burn these pois'nous weeds in yon blue fire,
These screech-owl's feathers and this prickling briar;
This cypress gathered at a dead man's grave;
That all thy fears and cares an end may have.

Then come, you Fairies, dance with me a round;
Melt her hard heart with your melodious sound:
In vain are all the charms I can devise:
She hath an art to break them with her eyes.

THOMAS CAMPION (1567–1620)   49

SONG

Choose now among this fairest number,
Upon whose breasts love would for ever slumber:
Choose not amiss since you may where you will,
    Or blame yourself for choosing ill.
Then do not leave, though oft the music closes,
Till lilies in their cheeks be turn'd to roses.

50   WILLIAM BROWNE OF TAVISTOCK
     (? 1590–1645)

ES STEHEN UNBEWEGLICH

The stars, for many ages,
Have dwelt in heaven above;
They gaze at one another
Tormented by their love.

They speak the richest language,
The loveliest ever heard;
Yet none of all the linguists
Can understand a word.

I learned it, though, in lessons
That nothing can erase;
The only text I needed
Was my beloved's face.

HEINRICH HEINE (1797–1856)   51
TRANS. AARON KRAMER

DU BIST WIE EINE BLUME

You're lovely as a flower,
So pure and fair to see;
I look at you, and sadness
Comes stealing over me.

I feel my hands should gently
Cover your head in prayer –
That God may always keep you
So lovely, pure and fair.

HEINRICH HEINE (1797–1856)
TRANS. AARON KRAMER

JUKE BOX LOVE SONG

I could take the Harlem night
and wrap around you,
Take the neon lights and make a crown,
Take the Lenox Avenue busses,
Taxis, subways,
And for your love song tone their rumble down.
Take Harlem's heartbeat,
Make a drumbeat,
Put it on a record, let it whirl,
And while we listen to it play,
Dance with you till day –
Dance with you, my sweet brown Harlem girl.

SINCE THE MAJORITY OF ME

Since the majority of me
Rejects the majority of you,
Debating ends forthwith, and we
Divide. And sure of what to do

We disinfect new blocks of days
For our majorities to rent
With unshared friends and unwalked ways.
But silence too is eloquent:

A silence of minorities
That, unopposed at last, return
Each night with cancelled promises
They want renewed. They never learn.

DID NOT

'Twas a new feeling – something more
Than we had dared to own before,
   Which then we hid not;
We saw it in each other's eye,
And wished, in every half-breathed sigh,
   To speak, but did not.

She felt my lips' impassioned touch –
'Twas the first time I dared so much,
   And yet she chid not;
But whispered o'er my burning brow,
'Oh! do you doubt I love you now?'
   Sweet soul! I did not.

Warmly I felt her bosom thrill,
I pressed it closer, closer still,
   Though gently bid not;
Till – oh! the world hath seldom heard
Of lovers, who so nearly erred,
   And yet, who did not.

THOMAS MOORE (1779–1852)

MY BELOVED IS MINE, AND I AM HIS;
HE FEEDETH AMONG THE LILLIES
(Canticles 11. 16)

Ev'n like two little bank-dividing brookes,
    That wash the pebles with their wanton streames,
And having rang'd and search'd a thousand nookes,
    Meet both at length in silver-brested *Thames*,
      Where in a greater Current they conjoyne:
So I my Best-Beloved's am; so He is mine.

Ev'n so we met; and after long pursuit,
    Ev'n so we joyn'd; we both became entire;
No need for either to renew a Suit,
    For I was Flax, and he was Flames of fire:
      Our firm-united souls did more than twine;
So I my Best-Beloved's am; so He is mine.

If all those glitt'ring Monarchs that command
    The servile Quarters of this earthly Ball,
Should tender, in Exchange, their shares of land,
    I would not change my Fortunes for them all:
      Their wealth is but a Counter to my Coyne:
The world's but theirs; but my Beloved's mine.

Nay more; If the fair Thespian Ladies all
    Should heap together their diviner treasure:

That Treasure should be deem'd a price too small
    To buy a minutes Lease of halfe my Pleasure.
        'Tis not the sacred wealth of all the Nine
Can buy my heart from Him, or His, from being mine.

Nor Time, nor Place, nor Chance, nor Death can bow
    My least desires unto the least remove;
He's firmly mine by Oath; I, His, by Vow;
    He's mine by Faith; and I am His by Love;
        He's mine by Water; I am His by Wine;
Thus I my Best-Beloved's am; thus He is mine.

He is my Altar; I, his Holy Place;
    I am his Guest; and he, my living Food;
I'm his, by Penitence; He, mine by Grace;
    I'm his, by Purchase; He is mine, by Blood;
        Hee's my supporting Elme, and I, his Vine:
Thus I my Best-Beloved's am; thus He is mine.

He gives me wealth, I give him all my Vowes:
    I give Him songs; He gives me length of dayes:
With wreathes of Grace he crownes my conqu'ring
        browes:
    And I, his Temples, with a Crowne of Praise,
        Which he accepts as an ev'rlasting signe,
That I my Best-Beloved's am; that He is mine.

FRANCIS QUARLES (1592–1644)   57

MEETING AND PASSING

As I went down the hill along the wall
There was a gate I had leaned at for the view
And had just turned from when I first saw you
As you came up the hill. We met. But all
We did that day was mingle great and small
Footprints in summer dust as if we drew
The figure of our being less than two
But more than one as yet. Your parasol
Pointed the decimal off with one deep thrust.
And all the time we talked you seemed to see
Something down there to smile at in the dust.
(Oh, it was without prejudice to me!)
Afterward I went past what you had passed
Before we met and you what I had passed.

THE CUCKOO

Cuckoos lead Bohemian lives,
They fail as husbands and as wives,
Therefore they cynically disparage
Everybody else's marriage.

OGDEN NASH (1902–1971)

MARRIAGE

Put your hand in the creel,
And draw an adder or an eel.

ANON.

WISH FOR A YOUNG WIFE

My lizard, my lively writher,
May your limbs never wither,
May the eyes in your face
Survive the green ice
Of envy's mean gaze;
May you live out your life
Without hate, without grief,
And your hair ever blaze,
In the sun, in the sun,
When I am undone,
When I am no one.

THE PURIST

I give you now Professor Twist,
A conscientious scientist.
Trustees exclaimed, 'He never bungles!'
And sent him off to distant jungles.
Camped on a tropic riverside,
One day he missed his loving bride.
She had, the guide informed him later,
Been eaten by an alligator.
Professor Twist could not but smile.
'You mean,' he said, 'a crocodile.'

OGDEN NASH (1902–1971)

IN PERSPECTIVE

What, keep love in *perspective*? – that old lie
Forced on the Imagination by the Eye
Which, mechanistically controlled, will tell
How rarely table-sides run parallel;
How distance shortens us; how wheels are found
Oval in shape far oftener than round;
How every ceiling-corner's out of joint;
How the broad highway tapers to a point –
Can all this fool us lovers? Not for long:
Even the blind will sense that something's wrong.

TO MY DEAR AND LOVING HUSBAND

If ever two were one, then surely we.
If ever man were lov'd by wife, then thee.
If ever wife was happy in a man,
Compare with me, ye woman, if you can.
I prize thy love more than whole mines of gold,
Or all the riches that the east doth hold.
My love is such that rivers cannot quench,
Nor ought but love from thee give recompence.
Thy love is such I can no way repay;
The heavens reward thee manifold I pray.
Then while we live, in love let's so perséver,
That when we love no more, we may live ever.

ANNE BRADSTREET (?1613—1672)

LIVING WITH A WIFE

At the Piano

Barefoot in purple pants
and my ski sweater you
play the piano most seriously
Mozart fumbled with a grimace
the lamplight fumbling unfelt
in the down of your neck

Kind field from which my progeny
have fled to grow voices and fangs
you are an arena where art
like a badly killed bull swerves again

Your bare foot lifts
the lamplight pedals on
my house is half music
my wife holds no harm

FIRELIGHT

Ten years together without yet a cloud,
They seek each other's eyes at intervals
Of gratefulness to firelight and four walls
For love's obliteration of the crowd.
Serenely and perennially endowed
And bowered as few may be, their joy recalls
No snake, no sword; and over them there falls
The blessing of what neither says aloud.

Wiser for silence, they were not so glad
Were she to read the graven tale of lines
On the wan face of one somewhere alone;
Nor were they more content could he have had
Her thoughts a moment since of one who shines
Apart, and would be hers if he had known.

E. A. ROBINSON (1869–1935)   65

ONE FLESH

Lying apart now, each in a separate bed,
He with a book, keeping the light on late,
She like a girl dreaming of childhood,
All men elsewhere – it is as if they wait
Some new event: the book he holds unread,
Her eyes fixed on the shadows overhead.

Tossed up like flotsam from a former passion,
How cool they lie. They hardly ever touch,
Or if they do it is like a confession
Of having little feeling – or too much.
Chastity faces them, a destination
For which their whole lives were a preparation.

Strangely apart, yet strangely close together,
Silence between them like a thread to hold
And not wind in. And time itself's a feather
Touching them gently. Do they know they're old,
These two who are my father and my mother
Whose fire from which I came, has now grown cold?

HIS AND HERS

Mornings weaving through the mud
Gave his high boots a cracked glory,
And she, crying where she stood,
Heard the hardly bothered-with story;
Each not knowing that pain clings
To the cleaned surface of things.

The greenhouse overspored with seeds
And the motor mower dried of oil,
Over the garage virginia creeper bleeds,
The lawn has patches of bare soil –
This is the Estate Agent's concern
Since he's in a box and she in an urn.

Behind a door missed by visitors
High boots and binoculars stand –
The arrogance his, the unhappiness hers;
Neither can get the upper hand,
The doing and the watching part
Outliving the torments of the heart.

PETER PORTER (b. 1929)   67

NOTHING BUT NO AND I

Nothing but no and I, and I and no,
How falls it out so strangely you reply?
I tell ye, fair, I'll not be answered so,
With this affirming no, denying I.
I say, I love, you sleightly answer, I:
I say, you love, you pule me out a no:
I say, I die, you echo me with I:
Save me, I cry, you sigh me out a no;

Must woe and I have nought but no and I?
No I am I, if I no more can have;
Answer no more, with silence make reply,
And let me take myself what I do crave,
   Let no and I, with I and you be so:
   Then answer no and I, and I and no.

DANCING FLAME

Pass now in metaphor beyond birds,
Their seasonal nesting and migration,
Their airy gambols, their repetitive song;
Beyond the puma and the ocelot
That spring in air and follow us with their eyes;
Beyond all creatures but our own selves,
Eternal genii of dancing flame
Armed with the irreproachable secret
Of love, which is: never to turn back.

ROBERT GRAVES (1895–1985)   69

WRESTLING

Our oneness is the wrestlers', fierce and close,
    Thrusting and thrust;
One life in dual effort for one prize, –
    We fight, and must;
For soul with soul does battle evermore
    Till love be trust.

Our distance is love's severance; sense divides,
    Each is but each;
Never the very hidden spirit of thee
    My life doth reach;
Twain! since love athwart the gulf that needs
    Kisses and speech.

Ah! wrestle closelier! we draw nearer so
    Than any bliss
Can bring twain souls who would be whole and one,
    Too near to kiss:
To be one thought, one voice before we die, –
    Wrestle for this.

70   LOUISA S. BEVINGTON (1845–?)

MARRIAGE COUNSEL

WHY MARRY OGRE
JUST TO GET A HUBBY
– headline in the Boston *Herald*

Why marry ogre
   Just to get hubby?
Has he a brogue, or
   Are his legs stubby?

Smokes he a stogie?
   Is he not sober?
Is he too logy
   And dull as a crowbar?

Tom, Dick, and Harry:
   Garrulous, greedy,
And grouchy. They vary
   From savage to seedy,

And, once wed, will parry
   To be set asunder.
O harpy, why marry
   Ogre? I wonder.

JOHN UPDIKE (b. 1932)

MIT DEINEN BLAUEN AUGEN

You gaze upon me sweetly
With your eyes of blue,
And my brain becomes so dreamy,
That I've no words for you.

I think about your blue eyes
Wherever I may be –
Over my heart are rolling
Blue thoughts like a sea.

HEINRICH HEINE (1797–1856)
TRANS. AARON KRAMER

PERSWASIONS TO ENJOY

If the quick spirits in your eye
Now languish, and anon must dye;
If every sweet, and every grace,
Must fly from that forsaken face:
   Then (*Celia*) let us reape our joyes
   E're time such goodly fruit destroyes.

Or, if that golden fleece must grow
For ever, free from aged snow;
If those bright Suns must know no shade,
Nor your fresh beauties ever fade:
Then feare not (*Celia*) to bestow,
What still being gather'd, still must grow.
   Thus, either *Time* his Sickle brings
   In vaine, or else in vaine his wings.

THE SNAPPED THREAD

Desire, first, by a natural miracle
United bodies, united hearts, blazed beauty;
Transcended bodies, transcended hearts.

Two souls, now unalterably one
In whole love always and for ever,
Soar out of twilight, through upper air,
Let fall their sensuous burden.

Is it kind, though, is it honest even,
To consort with none but spirits –
Leaving true-wedded hearts like ours
In enforced night-long separation,
Each to its random bodily inclination,
The thread of miracle snapped?

BLEST, BLEST AND HAPPY HE

Blest, blest and happy he
Whose eyes behold her face,
But blessed more whose ears hath heard
The speeches framed with grace.

And he is half a god
That these thy lips may kiss,
Yet god all whole that may enjoy
    Thy body as it is.

ANON.

IM WUNDERSCHÖNEN MONAT MAI

In May, the magic month of May,
When all the buds were breaking,
Oh then within my heart
The fires of love awakened.

In May, the magic month of May,
When birds were merry-making,
Oh then I told my darling
Of how my heart was aching.

76   HEINRICH HEINE (1797–1856)
TRANS. AARON KRAMER

BY TOO LONG GAZING ON
YOUR FLAWLESS FACE

By too long gazing on your flawless face
    my heart took fire, which such a heat dispersed
    that with a drought my lips were like to burst,
and speech itself was banished from its place.
You bad them bring well-water of your grace
    in a bejewelled vase, but, in my thirst,
        I brushed the spot which drinking you brushed
            first
still royal with your aromatic trace.
And well I knew the moment that I smutched it
    with mine, the vase, enamoured with your kiss,
and to the flame subdued whose splendour touched it,
    as in a furnace, was consumed with this.
How could I hope to rule my own desire,
when on the instant water changed to fire?

PIERRE DE RONSARD (1524–1585)   77
TRANS. HUMBERT WOLFE

THE NINTH SECRET POEM

I worship your fleece which is the perfect triangle
>   Of the Goddess
I am the lumberjack of the only virgin forest
>   O my Eldorado
I am the only fish in your voluptuous ocean
>   You my lovely Siren
I am the climber on your snowy mountains
>   O my whitest Alp
I am the heavenly archer of your beautiful mouth
>   O my darling quiver
I am the hauler of your midnight hair
>   O lovely ship on the canal of my kisses
And the lilies of your arms are beckoning me
>   O my summer garden
The fruits of your breast are ripening their honey for me
>   O my sweet-smelling orchard
And I am raising you O Madeleine O my beauty above
>   the earth
>   Like the torch of all light

78   GUILLAUME APOLLINAIRE (1880–1918)
TRANS. OLIVER BERNARD

FULL MANY A GLORIOUS MORNING
HAVE I SEEN

Full many a glorious morning have I seen
Flatter the mountain-tops with sovereign eye,
Kissing with golden face the meadows green,
Gilding pale streams with heavenly alchemy;
Anon permit the basest clouds to ride
With ugly rack on his celestial face,
And from the forlorn world his visage hide,
Stealing unseen to west with this disgrace:
Even so my sun one early morn did shine
With all-triumphant splendour on my brow;
But, out, alack! he was but one hour mine,
The region cloud hath maskt him from me now.
   Yet him for this my love no whit disdaineth;
   Suns of the world may stain when heaven's
     sun staineth.

WILLIAM SHAKESPEARE (1564–1616)

FROM THE BACK OF THE ROOM

From the back of the room, the bed, only a pallor spread,
the starry window surrendering to the greedy window
           announcing the day.
But here comes the one who hurries, who leans, and stays
after night's abandonment, it's this new and heavenly
           girl's turn to say yes!

At nothing else in the morning sky, the tender lover
           stares
at nothing but the enormous example of the sky himself:
           the heights and depths!
Only doves making round arenas in the air,
where their flight flashing in soft arcs parades
           a return of gentleness.

RAINER MARIA RILKE (1875–1926)
    TRANS. A. POULIN JR.

BOLDNESSE IN LOVE

Marke how the bashfull morne, in vaine
Courts the amorous Marigold,
With sighing blasts, and weeping raine;
Yet she refuses to unfold.
But when the Planet of the day,
Approacheth with his powerfull ray,
Then she spreads, then she receives
His warmer beames into her virgin leaves.
So shalt thou thrive in love, fond Boy;
If thy teares, and sighes discover
Thy griefe, thou never shalt enjoy
The just reward of a bold lover:
But when with moving accents, thou
Shalt constant faith, and service vow,
Thy *Celia* shall receive those charmes
With open eares, and with unfolded armes.

A SHALLOT

The full cloves
Of your buttocks, the convex
Curve of your belly, the curved
Cleft of your sex –

Out of this corm
That's planted in strong thighs
The slender stem and radiant
Flower rise.

DOCH DIE KASTRATEN KLAGTEN

And still the eunuchs grumbled,
   Whene'er my voice arose;
They grumbled as they mumbled
   My songs were far too gross.

And, oh, how sweetly thrilling
   Their little voices were;
Their light and limpid trilling
   Made such a pretty stir.

They sang of love, the leaping
   Flood that engulfs the heart...
The ladies all were weeping
   At such a feast of art!

HEINRICH HEINE (1797–1856)
TRANS. LOUIS UNTERMEYER

JAPANESE FAN

Though to talk too much of Heaven
    Is not well,
Though agreeable people never
    Mention Hell,
Yet the woman who betrayed me,
    Whom I kissed,
In that bygone summer taught me
    Both exist.
I was ardent, she was always
    Wisely cool,
So my lady played the traitor –
    I, the fool.
Oh! your pardon! but remember
    If you please,
I'm translating: this is only
    Japanese.

SONG

Why so pale and wan fond Lover?
   Prithee why so pale?
Will, when looking well can't move her,
   Looking ill prevaile?
   Prithee why so pale?

Why so dull and mute young Sinner?
   Prithee why so mute?
Will, when speaking well can't win her,
   Saying nothing doo't?
   Prithee why so mute?

Quit, quit, for shame, this will not move,
   This will not take her;
If of her selfe she will not Love,
   Nothing can make her:
   The Devill take her.

SIR JOHN SUCKLING (1609–1642)   85

ICH LIEBE SOLCHE WEISSE GLIEDER

I love this white and slender body,
   These limbs that answer love's caresses,
Passionate eyes, and forehead covered
   With a wave of thick, black tresses.

You are the very one I've searched for
   In many lands, in every weather.
You are my sort; you understand me;
   As equals we can talk together.

In me you've found the man you care for.
   And, for a while, you'll richly pay me
With kindness, kisses, and endearments –
   And then, as usual, you'll betray me.

HEINRICH HEINE (1797–1856)
TRANS. LOUIS UNTERMEYER

TWO RURAL SISTERS

Alice is tall and upright as a pine,
White as blanch'd almonds, or the falling snow,
Sweet as the damask roses when they blow,
And doubtless fruitful as the swelling vine.
Ripe to be cut, and ready to be press'd,
Her full cheek'd beauties very well appear,
And a year's fruit she loses ev'ry year,
Wanting a man to improve her to the best.

Full fain she would be husbanded, and yet,
Alas! she cannot a fit Lab'rer get
To cultivate her to her own content:
Fain would she be (God wot) about her task,
And yet (forsooth) she is too proud to ask,
And (which is worse) too modest to consent.

Marg'ret of humbler stature by the head
Is (as it oft falls out with yellow hair)
Than her fair sister, yet so much more fair,
As her pure white is better mixt with red.
This, hotter than the other ten to one,
Longs to be put into her mother's trade,
And loud proclaims she lives too long a maid,
wishing for one t'untie her virgin zone.

She finds virginity a kind of ware,
That's very very troublesome to bear,
And being gone, she thinks will ne'er be mist:
And yet withal, the girl has so much grace,
To call for help I know she wants the face,
Though ask'd, I know not how she would resist.

SONG

Love a woman? You're an ass!
   'Tis a most insipid passion
To choose out for your happiness
   The silliest part of God's creation.

Let the porter and the groom,
   Things designed for dirty slaves,
Drudge in fair Aurelia's womb
   To get supplies for age and graves.

Farewell, woman! I intend
   Henceforth every night to sit
With my lewd, well-natured friend,
   Drinking to engender wit.

Then give me health, wealth, mirth, and wine,
   And, if busy love entrenches,
There's a sweet, soft page of mine
   Does the trick worth forty wenches.

JOHN WILMOT, EARL OF ROCHESTER   89
(1647–1680)

FATIGUE

I'm tired of Love: I'm still more tired of Rhyme.
But Money gives me pleasure all the time.

UNFORTUNATE COINCIDENCE

By the time you swear you're his,
Shivering and sighing,
And he vows his passion is
Infinite, undying –
Lady, make a note of this:
One of you is lying.

DOROTHY PARKER (1893–1967)   91

SOCIAL NOTE

Lady, lady, should you meet
One whose ways are all discreet,
One who murmurs that his wife
Is the lodestar of his life,
One who keeps assuring you
That he never was untrue,
Never loved another one...
Lady, lady, better run!

WOMAN AND TREE

To love one woman, or to sit
    Always beneath the same tall tree,
Argues a certain lack of wit
    Two steps from imbecility.

A poet, therefore, sworn to feed
    On every food the senses know,
Will claim the inexorable need
    To be Don Juan Tenorio.

Yet if, miraculously enough,
    (And why set miracles apart?)
Woman and tree prove of a stuff
    Wholly to glamour his wild heart?

And if such visions from the void
    As shone in fever there, or there,
Assemble, hold and are enjoyed
    On climbing one familiar stair . . . ?

To change and chance he took a vow,
    As he thought fitting. None the less,
What of a phoenix on the bough,
    Or a sole woman's fatefulness?

ROBERT GRAVES (1895–1985)   93

IN A BATH TEASHOP

'Let us not speak, for the love we bear one another –
      Let us hold hands and look.'
She, such a very ordinary little woman;
      He, such a thumping crook;
But both, for a moment, little lower than the angels
      In the teashop's ingle-nook.

THE OTHER

What is she, while I live? –
Who plagues me with her Shape,
Lifting a nether Lip
Lightly: so buds unleave;
But if I move too close,
Who busks me on the Nose?

Is she what I become?
Is this my final Face?
I find her every place;
She happens, time on time –
My Nose feels for my Toe;
Nature's too much to know.

Who can surprise a thing
Or come to love alone?
A lazy natural man,
I loll, I loll, all Tongue.
She moves, and I adore:
Motion can do no more.

A child stares past a fire
With the same absent gaze:
I know her careless ways! –
Desire hides from desire.
Aging, I sometimes weep,
Yet still laugh in my sleep.

THEODORE ROETHKE (1908–1963)   95

PARTICULAR YOU

    What question will unmask
The hooded rose-tree, upright in its shadow?
Or show the steadiness that makes the stone steady?
    Or, knowing it, who would dare to ask
And change the pretty phenomena into one
Horde of disclosures blackening the sun?

    Reveal to me no more
Than what I know of you – your bright disguises.
The lie your body is only discloses
    The language of a rose-tree or
A stone; and universals gather where
Your hands lie still or light falls on your hair.

    But you are more and less
Than universals. I'd tremble to discover
That special, stubborn thing, that must forever
    Lie hooded between no and yes,
An affirmation which must always be
Incomprehensible and separate from me.

I study to be wise.
Lift up the lesson of your hand. Then, gazing,
I lose the loss of what I must be losing
    And find the language of disguise
Says all I want and bear to know, that we
And all the world are three, but one in three.

LOVE UNDER THE REPUBLICANS
(OR DEMOCRATS)

Come live with me and be my love
And we will all the pleasures prove
Of a marriage conducted with economy
In the Twentieth Century Anno Donomy.
We'll live in a dear little walk-up flat
With practically room to swing a cat
And a potted cactus to give it hauteur
And a bathtub equipped with dark brown water.
We'll eat, without undue discouragement,
Foods low in cost but high in nouragement
And quaff with pleasure, while chatting wittily,
The peculiar wine of Little Italy.
We'll remind each other it's smart to be thrifty
And buy our clothes for something-fifty.
We'll stand in line on holidays
For seats at unpopular matinees
For every Sunday we'll have a lark
And take a walk in Central Park.
And one of these days not too remote
I'll probably up and cut your throat.

NOT MINE OWN FEARS, NOR THE PROPHETIC SOUL

Not mine own fears, nor the prophetic soul
Of the wide world dreaming on things to come,
Can yet the lease of my true love control,
Supposed as forfeit to a confined doom.
The mortal moon hath her eclipse endured,
And the sad augurs mock their own presage;
Incertainties now crown themselves assured,
And peace proclaims olives of endless age.
Now with the drops of this most balmy time
My love looks fresh, and Death to me subscribes,
Since, spite of him, I'll live in this poor rime,
While he insults o'er dull and speechless tribes:
    And thou in this shalt find thy monument,
    When tyrants' crests and tombs of brass are spent.

THE AZALEA

There, where the sun shines first
Against our room,
She train'd the gold Azalea, whose perfume
She, Spring-like, from her breathing grace dispersed.
Last night the delicate crests of saffron bloom,
For this their dainty likeness watch'd and nurst,
Were just at point to burst.
At dawn I dream'd, O God, that she was dead,
And groan'd aloud upon my wretched bed,
And waked, ah, God, and did not waken her,
But lay, with eyes still closed,
Perfectly bless'd in the delicious sphere
By which I knew so well that she was near,
My heart to speechless thankfulness composed.
Till 'gan to stir
A dizzy somewhat in my troubled head –
It *was* the azalea's breath, and she *was* dead!
The warm night had the lingering buds disclosed,
And I had fall'n asleep with to my breast
A chance-found letter press'd
In which she said,
'So, till to-morrow eve, my Own, adieu!
Parting's well-paid with soon again to meet,
Soon in your arms to feel so small and sweet,
Sweet to myself that am so sweet to you!'

THE WAY I READ A LETTER'S THIS

The way I read a letter's this:
'Tis first I lock the door,
And push it with my fingers next,
For transport it be sure.

And then I go the furthest off
To counteract a knock;
Then draw my little letter forth
And softly pick its lock.

Then, glancing narrow at the wall,
And narrow at the floor,
For firm conviction of a mouse
Not exorcised before,

Peruse how infinite I am
To – no one that you know!
And sigh for lack of heaven, – but not
The heaven the creeds bestow.

AN APPEAL TO CATS IN
THE BUSINESS OF LOVE

Ye cats that at midnight spit love at each other,
Who best feel the pangs of a passionate lover,
I appeal to your scratches and your tattered fur,
If the business of Love be no more than to purr.
Old Lady Grimalkin with her gooseberry eyes,
Knew something when a kitten, for why she is wise;
You find by experience, the love-fit's soon o'er,
Puss! Puss! lasts not long, but turns to *Cat-whore!*
    Men ride many miles,
    Cats tread many tiles,
  Both hazard their necks in the fray;
    Only cats, when they fall
    From a house or a wall,
  Keep their feet, mount their tails, and away!

CAT-GODDESSES

A perverse habit of cat-goddesses –
Even the blackest of them, black as coals
Save for a new moon blazing on each breast,
With coral tongues and beryl eyes like lamps,
Long leggèd, pacing three by three in nines –
This obstinate habit is to yield themselves,
In verisimilar love-ecstasies,
To tatter-eared and slinking alley-toms
No less below the common run of cats
Than they above it; which they do for spite,
To provoke jealousy – not the least abashed
By such gross-headed, rabbit-coloured litters
As soon they shall be happy to desert.

ROBERT GRAVES (1895–1985)

CYNTHIA ON HORSEBACK

Fair Cynthia mounted on her sprightly pad,
Which in white robe with silver fringe was clad,
    And swift as wind his graceful steps did move,
    As with his beauteous guide he'd been in love.
Though fierce, yet humble still to her command,
Obeying ev'ry touch of her fair hand;
    Her golden bit his foaming mouth did check,
    It spread his crest, and rais'd his bending neck.

She was the rose upon this hill of snow,
Her sparkling beauty made this glorious show;
    Whence secret flames men in their bosoms took:
The Graces and the Cupids her surround,
Attending her, while cruel she does wound,
    With switch her horse, and hearts with ev'ry look.

THE DEFIANCE

By Heaven 'tis false, I am not vain;
    And rather would the subject be
Of your indifference, or disdain,
    Than wit or raillery.

Take back the trifling praise you give,
    And pass it on some other fool,
Who may the injuring wit believe,
    That turns her into ridicule.

Tell her, she's witty, fair, and gay,
    With all the charms that can subdue:
Perhaps she'll credit what you say;
    But curse me if I do.

If your diversion you design,
    On my good-nature you have prest:
Or if you do intend it mine,
    You have mistook the jest.

APHRA BEHN (1640–1689)

THE APPARITION

When by thy scorn, O murd'ress, I am dead,
    And that thou thinkst thee free
From all solicitation from me,
Then shall my ghost come to thy bed,
And thee, fain'd vestal, in worse arms shall see;
Then thy sick taper will begin to wink,
And he, whose thou art then, being tir'd before,
Will, if thou stir, or pinch to wake him, think
    Thou call'st for more,
And in false sleep will from thee shrink,
And then poor aspen wretch, neglected thou
Bath'd in a cold quicksilver sweat wilt lie
A verier ghost than I;
What I will say, I will not tell thee now,
Lest that preserve thee; and since my love is spent,
I had rather thou shouldst painfully repent,
Than by my threat'nings rest still innocent.

STILL TO BE NEAT

Still to be neat, still to be drest,
As you were going to a feast;
Still to be powder'd, still perfum'd:
Lady, it is to be presum'd,
Though art's hid causes are not found,
All is not sweet, all is not sound.

Give me a look, give me a face,
That makes simplicity a grace;
Robes loosely flowing, hair as free:
Such sweet neglect more taketh me
Than all th'adulteries of art.
They strike mine eyes, but not my heart.

BEN JONSON (1572/3-1637)

TO MY INCONSTANT MISTRIS

When thou, poore excommunicate
    From all the joyes of love, shalt see
The full reward, and glorious fate,
    Which my strong faith shall purchase me,
    Then curse thine owne inconstancie.

A fayrer hand than thine, shall cure
    That heart, which thy false oathes did wound;
And to my soule, a soule more pure
    Than thine, shall by Loves hand be bound,
    And both with equall glory crown'd.

Then shalt thou weepe, entreat, complaine
    To Love, as I did once to thee;
When all thy teares shall be as vaine
    As mine were then, for thou shalt bee
    Damn'd for thy false Apostasie.

TO A LADY MAKING LOVE

Good madam, when ladies are willing,
   A man must needs look like a fool;
For me I would not give a shilling
   For one who would love out of rule.

You should leave us to guess by your blushing,
   And not speak the matter so plain;
'Tis our's to write and be pushing,
'Tis yours to affect disdain.

That you're in a terrible taking,
   By all these sweet oglings I see,
But the fruit that can fall without shaking,
   Indeed is too mellow for me.

LADY MARY WORTLEY MONTAGU   109
(1689–1762)

SATAN, NO WOMAN, YET
A WANDERING SPIRIT

Satan, no woman, yet a wandering spirit,
When he saw ships sail two ways with one wind,
Of sailors' trade he hell did disinherit:
The Devil himself loves not a half-fast mind.

The satyr when he saw the shepherd blow
To warm his hands, and make his pottage cool,
Manhood forswears, and half a beast did know,
Nature with double breath is put to school.

Cupid doth head his shafts in women's faces,
Where smiles and tears dwell ever near together,
Where all the arts of change give passion graces;
While these clouds threaten, who fears not
        the weather?
    Sailors and satyrs, Cupid's knights, and I,
    Fear women that swear, Nay; and know they lie.

THE TREE IN PAMELA'S GARDEN

Pamela was too gentle to deceive
Her roses. 'Let the men stay where they are,'
She said, 'and if Apollo's avatar
Be one of them, I shall not have to grieve.'
And so she made all Tilbury Town believe
She sighed a little more for the North Star
Than over men, and only in so far
As she was in a garden was like Eve.

Her neighbors – doing all that neighbors can
To make romance of reticence meanwhile –
Seeing that she had never loved a man,
Wished Pamela had a cat, or a small bird,
And only would have wondered at her smile
Could they have seen that she had overheard.

E. A. ROBINSON (1869–1935)

THE BACHELOR'S SONG

How happy a thing were a wedding
    And a bedding,
If a man might purchase a wife
   For a twelvemonth and a day;
But to live with her all a man's life,
   For ever and for ay,
Till she grow as grey as a cat,
Good faith, Mr Parson, I thank you for that.

IF YOU DON'T LIKE MY APPLES

If you don't like my apples,
    Don't shake my tree.
I'm not after your boy friend,
    He's after me.

ANON.

APPLES BE RIPE

Apples be ripe
And nuts be brown,
Petticoats up
And trousers down.

ANON.

WIR STANDEN AN DER STRASSENECK

We stood upon the corner, where,
    For upwards of an hour,
We spoke with soulful tenderness
    Of love's transcending power.

Our fervors grew; a hundred times
    Impassioned oaths we made there.
We stood upon the corner – and,
    Alas, my love, we stayed there!

The goddess Opportunity,
    A maid, alert and sprightly,
Came by, observed us standing there,
    And passed on, laughing lightly.

THE STARRED COVERLET

A difficult achievement for true lovers
Is to lie mute, without embrace or kiss,
Without a rustle or a smothered sigh,
Basking each in the other's glory.

Let us not undervalue lips or arms
As reassurances of constancy,
Or speech as necessary communication
When troubled hearts go groping through the dusk;

Yet lovers who have learned this last refinement –
To lie apart, yet sleep and dream together
Motionless under their starred coverlet –
Crown love with wreaths of myrtle.

ROBERT GRAVES (1895–1985)   115

TO HIS MISTRESS, OBJECTING TO HIM NEITHER TOYING NOR TALKING

You say I love not, 'cause I do not play
   Still with your curls, and kiss the time away.
   You blame me, too, becaue I can't devise
   Some sport to please those babies in your eyes; –
By Love's religion, I must here confess it,
   The most I love, when I the least express it.
   Small griefs find tongues; full casks are ever found
   To give, if any, yet but little sound.
Deep waters noiseless are; and this we know,
   That chiding streams betray small depth below.
   So when love speechless is, she doth express
   A depth in love, and that depth bottomless.
Now, since my love is tongueless, know me such,
   Who speak but little, 'cause I love so much.

TO MY VALENTINE

More than a catbird hates a cat,
Or a criminal hates a clue,
Or the Axis hates the United States,
That's how much I love you.

I love you more than a duck can swim,
And more than a grapefruit squirts,
I love you more than gin rummy is a bore,
And more than a toothache hurts.

As a shipwrecked sailor hates the sea,
Or a juggler hates a shove,
As a hostess detests unexpected guests,
That's how much you I love.

I love you more than a wasp can sting,
And more than the subway jerks,
I love you as much as a beggar needs a crutch,
And more than a hangnail irks.

I swear to you by the stars above,
And below, if such there be,
As the High Court loathes perjurious oaths,
That's how you're loved by me.

OGDEN NASH (1902–1971)   117

SONNET

Tell me no more how fair she is,
    I have no minde to hear
The story of that distant bliss
    I never shall come near:
By sad experience I have found
That her perfection is my wound.

And tell me not how fond I am
    To tempt a daring Fate,
From whence no triumph ever came,
    But to repent too late:
There is some hope ere long I may
In silence dote my self away.

I ask no pity (Love) from thee,
    Not will thy justice blame,
So that thou wilt not envy mee
    The glory of my flame:
Which crowns my heart when ere it dyes,
In that it falls her sacrifice.

SILLY BOY, 'TIS FULL MOON YET

Silly boy, 'tis full moon yet, thy night as day
    shines clearly;
Had thy youth but wit to fear, thou couldst not
    love so dearly.
Shortly wilt thou mourn when all thy pleasures
    are bereaved;
Little knows he how to love that never was
    deceived.

This is thy first maiden flame, that triumphs yet
    unstained;
All is artless now you speak, not one word yet is
    fained;
All is heav'n that you behold, and all your
    thoughts are blessed:
But no Spring can want his Fall, each Troilus hath
    his Cressid.

Thy well-order'd locks ere long shall rudely hang
    neglected;
And thy lively pleasant cheer read grief on earth
    dejected.
Much then wilt thou blame thy Saint, that made
    thy heart so holy,
And with sighs confess, in love, that too much
    faith is folly.

Yet, be just and constant still; Love may beget a
    wonder,
Not unlike a Summer's frost, or Winter's fatal
    thunder:
He that holds his sweetheart true unto his day of
    dying
Lives, of all that ever breath'd, most worthy the
    envying.

THIS LUNAR BEAUTY

This lunar beauty
Has no history,
Is complete and early;
If beauty later
Bear any feature
It had a lover
And is another.

This like a dream
Keeps other time,
And daytime is
The loss of this;
For time is inches
And the heart's changes
Where ghost has haunted,
Lost and wanted.

But this was never
A ghost's endeavour
Nor, finished this,
Was ghost at ease;
And till it pass
Love shall not near
The sweetness here
Nor sorrow take
His endless look.

W. H. AUDEN (1907–1973)

HOW MANY PALTRY, FOOLISH, PAINTED THINGS

How many paltry, foolish, painted things,
  That now in coaches trouble every street,
Shall be forgotten, whom no poet sings,
  Ere they be well wrapped in their winding-sheet?
Where I to thee eternity shall give,
  When nothing else remaineth of these days,
And Queens hereafter shall be glad to live
  Upon the alms of thy superfluous praise.
Virgins and matrons, reading these my rhymes,
  Shall be so much delighted with thy story,
That they shall grieve they lived not in these times,
  To have seen thee, their sex's only glory.
    So shalt thou fly above the vulgar throng,
    Still to survive in my immortal song.

INSOMNIA

The moon in the bureau mirror
looks out a million miles
(and perhaps with pride, at herself,
but she never, never smiles)
far and away beyond sleep, or
perhaps she's a daytime sleeper.

By the Universe deserted,
she'd tell it to go to hell,
and she'd find a body of water,
or a mirror, on which to dwell.
So wrap up care in a cobweb
and drop it down the well

into that world inverted
where left is always right,
where the shadows are really the body,
where we stay awake all night,
where the heavens are shallow as the sea
is now deep, and you love me.

THE CHANGE

Love in her sunny Eyes doth basking play;
Love walks the pleasant Mazes of her Haire;
Love does on both her Lipps for ever stray;
And sowes and reapes a thousand kisses there.
In all her outward parts Love's always seene;
    But, oh, Hee never went within.

Within Loves foes, his greatest foes abide,
    Malice, Inconstancy and Pride.
Soe the Earths face, Trees, Herbes, and Flowers
        do dresse;
    With other beauties numberlesse:
But at the Center Darknesse is, and Hell;
There wicked Spirits, and there the Damned dwell.

With Me alas, quite contrary it fares;
Darkness and Death lyes in my weeping eyes,
Despaire and Palenesse in my face appears,
And Griefe, and Fear, Loves greatest enemies;
But, like the Persian Tyrant, Love within
    Keeps his proud Court, and ne're is seen.

Oh take my Heart, and by that means you'l prove
    Within too stor'd enough of Love:
Give me but Yours, I'le by that change so thrive
    That Love in all my parts shall live.
So powerfull is this change, it render can,
My outside Woman, and your inside Man.

ABRAHAM COWLEY (1618–1667)   125

IF YOU WERE COMING
IN THE FALL

If you were coming in the fall,
I'd brush the summer by
With half a smile and half a spurn,
As housewives do a fly.

If I could see you in a year,
I'd wind the months in balls,
And put them each in separate drawers,
Until their time befalls.

If only centuries delayed,
I'd count them on my hand,
Subtracting till my fingers dropped
Into Van Diemen's land.

If certain, when this life was out,
That yours and mine should be,
I'd toss it yonder like a rind,
And taste eternity.

But now, all ignorant of the length
Of time's uncertain wing,
It goads me, like the goblin bee,
That will not state its sting.

WHEN IN THE CHRONICLE
OF WASTED TIME

When in the chronicle of wasted time
I see descriptions of the fairest wights,
And beauty making beautiful old rime
In praise of ladies dead and lovely knights,
Then, in the blazon of sweet beauty's best,
Of hand, of foot, of lip, of eye, of brow,
I see their antique pen would have exprest
Even such a beauty as you master now.
So all their praises are but prophecies
Of this our time, all you prefiguring;
And, for they lookt but with divining eyes,
They had not skill enough your worth to sing:
    For we, which now behold these present days,
    Have eyes to wonder, but lack tongues to praise.

SILVER BIRCH

A silver birch dances at my window.
The faint clouds dimly seen
On the sloped azure are easy to be scattered
When full day's wind sweeps clean.

Call to walk comes as of true nature,
Easy should the body move.
And poetry comes after eight miles' seeking,
Mere right out of mere love.

BEFORE THE WORLD WAS MADE

If I make the lashes dark
And the eyes more bright
And the lips more scarlet,
Or ask if all be right
From mirror after mirror,
No vanity's displayed:
I'm looking for the face I had
Before the world was made.

What if I look upon a man
As though on my beloved,
And my blood be cold the while
And my heart unmoved?
Why should he think me cruel
Or that he is betrayed?
I'd have him love the thing that was
Before the world was made.

W. B. YEATS (1865–1939)   129

OF YOUTH HE SINGETH

In a herber green asleep whereas I lay,
The birds sang sweet in the middes of the day;
I dreaměd fast of mirth and play:
      In youth is pleasure, in youth is pleasure.

Methought I walked still to and fro,
And from her company I could not go;
But when I waked it was not so:
      In youth is pleasure, in youth is pleasure.

Therefore, my heart is surely pight
Of her alone to have a sight,
Which is my joy and heart's delight:
      In youth is pleasure, in youth is pleasure.

BLACK CANDLE

It is your fate, for your narrow shoulders
    to turn red under the lashes,
red under the lashes, to burn in the frost,

for your childish hands to lift the iron,
to lift the iron and tie bundles,

for your tender bare feet to tread on glass,
to tread on glass and on the bloody sand.

And as for me, I burn after you like a black candle,
burn like a black candle and dare not pray.

OSIP MANDELSTAM (1891–?1938)
TRANS. RICHARD AND ELIZABETH McKANE

STOLEN PLEASURE

My sweet did sweetly sleep,
And on her rosy face
Stood tears of pearl, which beauty's self did weep;
I, wond'ring at her grace,
Did all amaz'd remain,
When Love said, 'Fool, can looks thy wishes crown?
Time past comes not again.'
Then did I me bow down,
And kissing her fair breast, lips, cheeks, and eyes,
Prov'd here on earth the joys of paradise.

KISSES DESIRED

Though I with strange desire
To kiss those rosy lips am set on fire,
Yet will I cease to crave
Sweet touches in such store,
As he who long before
From Lesbia them in thousands did receive.
Heart mine, but once me kiss,
And I by that sweet bliss
Even swear to cease you to importune more;
Poor one no number is;
Another word of me ye shall not hear
After one kiss, but still one kiss, my dear.

LATELY AS DREAMING ON A STAIR I STOOD

Lately as dreaming on a stair I stood
   you passed me by, and, looking on my face,
   blinded my eyes with the immediate grace
of unanticipated neighbourhood.
As lightning splits the clouds, my heart and blood
   split with your beauty, and began to race,
   now ice, now fever, shattered in their place
by that unparalleled beatitude.
And, if your hand, in passing, had not beckoned –
   your whiter hand than is the swan's white daughter,
   Helen, your eyes had wounded me to death.
But your hand saved me in the mortal second,
   and your triumphant eyes the moment after
   revived their captive with an alms of breath.

134   PIERRE DE RONSARD (1524–1585)
TRANS. HUMBERT WOLFE

MEDIOCRITIE IN LOVE REJECTED

Give me more love, or more disdaine;
   The Torrid, or the frozen Zone,
Bring equall ease unto my paine;
   The temperate affords me none:
Either extreame, of love, or hate,
Is sweeter than a calme estate.

Give me a storme; if it be love,
   Like *Danae* in that golden showre
I swimme in pleasure; if it prove
   Disdaine, that torrent will devoure
My Vulture-hopes; and he's possest
Of Heaven, that's but from Hell releast:
   Then crowne my joyes, or cure my paine;
   Give me more love, or more disdaine.

THOMAS CAREW (1594/5–1640)

TO A FAIR LADY, PLAYING
WITH A SNAKE

Strange! that such horror and such grace
Should dwell together in one place;
A fury's arm, an angel's face!

'Tis innocence, and youth, which makes
In Chloris' fancy such mistakes,
To start at love, and play with snakes.

By this and by her coldness barred,
Her servants have a task too hard;
The tyrant has a double guard!

Thrice happy snake! that in her sleeve
May boldly creep; we dare not give
Our thoughts so unconfined a leave.

Contented in that nest of snow
He lies, as he his bliss did know,
And to the wood no more would go.

Take heed, fair Eve! you do not make
Another tempter of this snake;
A marble one so warmed would speak.

TWO LOVES I HAVE
OF COMFORT AND DESPAIR

Two loves I have of comfort and despair,
Which like two spirits do suggest me still:
The better angel is a man right fair,
The worser spirit a woman colour'd ill.
To win me soon to hell, my female evil
Tempteth my better angel from my side,
And would corrupt my saint to be a devil,
Wooing his purity with her foul pride.
And whether that my angel be turn'd fiend
Suspect I may, yet not directly tell;
But being both from me, both to each friend,
I guess one angel in another's hell:
   Yet this shall I ne'er know, but live in doubt,
   Till my bad angel fire my good one out.

WILLIAM SHAKESPEARE (1564–1616)

DEAR, THOUGH THE NIGHT IS GONE

Dear, though the night is gone,
The dream still haunts to-day
That brought us to a room,
Cavernous, lofty as
A railway terminus,
And crowded in that gloom
Were beds, and we in one
In a far corner lay.

Our whisper woke no clocks,
We kissed and I was glad
At everything you did,
Indifferent to those
Who sat with hostile eyes
In pairs on every bed,
Arms round each other's necks,
Inert and vaguely sad.

O but what worm of guilt
Or what malignant doubt
Am I the victim of;
That you then, unabashed,
Did what I never wished,
Confessed another love;
And I, submissive, felt
Unwanted and went out?

THE LOVER COMPARETH HIS STATE TO
A SHIP IN PERILOUS STORM TOSSED
ON THE SEA

My galley, charged with forgetfulness,
Thorough sharp seas in winter nights doth pass
'Tween rock and rock; and eke my foe, alas,
That is my lord, steereth with cruelness;
And every oar a thought in readiness,
As though that death were light in such a case;
An endless wind doth tear the sail apace
Of forced sighs, and trusty fearfulness;
A rain of tears, a cloud of dark disdain,
Hath done the wearied cords great hinderance;
Wreathed with error and eke with ignorance,
The stars be hid that led me to this pain.
   Drowned is reason that should me comfort,
   And I remain, despairing of the port.

SIR THOMAS WYATT (1503–1542)   139

APOLLO THRUST HIS GOLDEN HEAD BETWEEN US

Apollo thrust his golden head between us
 athwart the lattice with your eyes engaging,
 but with the brilliant warfare he was waging
blinded withdrew, as though he ne'er had seen us.
Whenas I made him Vulcan to your Venus
 gazing with eyes that needed no assuaging,
 you softly cried, 'The jealous god is raging
because we two as lovers here demean us.'
At such a victory, so sweetly laurelled,
 Mars burned with an intolerable joy –
 alas! as it was unexpected, fleeting,
since I, who mocked the god with whom I quarrelled,
 for the brief graces of a scented boy
 was left the instant that he gave you greeting.

PIERRE DE RONSARD (1524–1585)
TRANS. HUMBERT WOLFE

ALTER?

Alter? When the hills do.
Falter? When the sun
Question if his glory
Be the perfect one.

Surfeit? When the daffodil
Doth of the dew:
Even as herself, O friend!
I will of you!

SIE LIEBTEN SICH BEIDE, DOCH KEINER

They were in love, but neither
Would let the other know;
And while they were dying of passion,
Hatred was all they'd show.

They parted at last, and only
In dream did their love live on.
Long ago they perished,
And scarcely knew they were gone.

THE BROKEN HEART
'Oh, Sing to me Gypsy.'

He told me he loved me,
He gave me red roses,
Twelve crimson roses
As red as my blood.

The roses he gave me,
The roses are withered,
Twelve crimson roses
As red as my blood.

The roses are withered,
But here on my breast, far
Redder than they is
The red of my heart's blood.

He told me he loved me,
He gave me red roses,
Twelve crimson roses
As red as my blood.

STEVIE SMITH (1902–1971)   143

A RED, RED ROSE

O my Luve's like a red, red rose,
 That's newly sprung in June;
O my Luve's like the melodie
 That's sweetly play'd in tune. –

As fair art thou, my bonie lass,
 So deep in luve am I;
And I will love thee still, my Dear,
 Till a' the seas gang dry. –

Till a' the seas gang dry, my Dear,
 And the rocks melt wi' the sun:
I will love thee still, my Dear,
 While the sands o' life shall run. –

And fare thee weel, my only Luve!
 And fare thee weel, a while!
And I will come again, my Luve,
 Tho' it were ten thousand mile! –

KIND ARE HER ANSWERS

      Kind are her answers,
But her performance keeps no day;
      Breaks time, as dancers
From their own music when they stray.
      All her free favours
And smooth words wing my hopes in vain.
O did ever voice so sweet but only feign?
Can true love yield such delay,
      Converting joy to pain?

      Lost is our freedom
When we submit to women so.
      Why do we need them
When in their best they work our woe?
      There is no wisdom
Can alter ends by Fate prefixed.
O why is the good of man with evil mixed?
Never were days yet called two,
      But one night went betwixt.

THOMAS CAMPION (1567–1620)

LOVE AND MURDER

Strange that in 'crimes of passion' what results
Is women folded into trunks like suits,
Or chopped in handy joints to burn or lose,
Or sallowed with poison, puffed with sea,
Or turned into waistless parcels and bestowed
Under the fuel or the kitchen floor.

Perhaps those ardent murderers so prize
The flesh that it disturbs them not at all
To separate an ankle with an axe,
Or contemplate some leathern lady, long
Of the spare bedroom pungent occupant.
Love, after all, must overcome disgust.

We lesser amorists make do with girls
Prim or unfaithful, loud and ageing wives.
Loving too little to implant them deep
Within our guilty dreams where secretly
They would take off their green and purple clothes
To show the unchanging shamelessness of bone.

YOU MUST NOT WONDER THOUGH
YOU THINK IT STRANGE

You must not wonder though you think it strange
To see me hold my lowring head so low,
And that mine eyes take no delight to range
About the gleams which on your face do grow.
The mouse which once hath broken out of trap
Is seldom tested with the trustless bait,
But lies aloof for fear of more mishap
And feedeth still in doubt of deep deceit.
The scorched fly which once hath 'scaped the flame
Will hardly come to play again with fire.
Whereby I learn that grievous is the game
Which follows fancy dazzled by desire.
   So that I wink or else hold down my head
   Because your blazing eyes my bale have bred.

GEORGE GASCOIGNE (*c.* 1525–1577)   147

SONNET. THE DOUBLE ROCK

Since thou hast view'd some Gorgon, and art grown
             A solid stone:
To bring again to softness thy hard heart
             Is past my art.
Ice may relent to water in a thaw;
But stone made flesh Loves Chymistry ne're saw.

Therefore by thinking on thy hardness, I
             Will petrify;
And so within our double Quarryes Wombe,
             Dig our Loves Tombe.
Thus strangely will our difference agree;
And with our selves, amaze the world, to see
How both Revenge and Sympathy consent
To make two Rocks each others Monument.

AUTUMN

He told his life story to Mrs Courtly
Who was a widow. 'Let us get married shortly',
He said. 'I am no longer passionate,
But we can have some conversation before it is
      too late.'

STEVIE SMITH (1902–1971)

UPON LOVE

Love brought me to a silent Grove,
   And shew'd me there a Tree,
Where some had hang'd themselves for love,
   And gave a Twist to me.

The Halter was of silk, and gold,
   That he reacht forth unto me:
No otherwise, than if he would
   By dainty things undo me.

He bade me then that Neck-lace use;
   And told me too, he maketh
A glorious end by such a Noose,
   His Death for Love that taketh.

'Twas but a dream; but had I been
   There really alone;
My desp'rate feares, in love, had seen
   Mine Execution.

ON HIS MISTRESS, THE QUEEN
OF BOHEMIA

You meaner beauties of the night,
    That poorly satisfy our eyes
More by your number than your light;
    You common people of the skies,
    What are you when the sun shall rise?

You curious chanters of the wood,
    That warble forth Dame Nature's lays,
Thinking your voices understood
    By your weak accents; what's your praise
When Philomel her voice shall raise?

You violets that first appear,
    By your pure purple mantles known,
Like the proud virgins of the year,
    As if the spring were all your own;
    What are you when the rose is blown?

So, when my Mistress shall be seen
    In form and beauty of her mind,
By virtue first, then choice, a Queen,
    Tell me, if she were not designed
    The eclipse and glory of her kind?

SIR HENRY WOTTON (1568–1639)   151

AN APOLOGY FOR HAVING LOVED BEFORE

They that never had the use
Of the grape's surprising juice,
To the first delicious cup
All their reason render up;
Neither do, nor care to know,
Whether it be best or no.

So they that are to love inclined
Swayed by chance, not choice, or art,
To the first that's fair, or kind,
Make a present of their heart;
'Tis not she that first we love,
But whom dying we approve.

To man, that was in the evening made,
Stars gave the first delight,
Admiring, in the gloomy shade,
Those little drops of light;
Then at Aurora, whose fair hand
Removed them from the skies,
He gazing toward the east did stand,
She entertained his eyes.

THAT SELF-SAME TONGUE WHICH
FIRST DID THEE ENTREAT

That self-same tongue which first did thee entreat
To link thy liking with my lucky love,
That trusty tongue must now these words repeat,
I love thee still, my fancy cannot move,
That dreadless heart which durst attempt the thought
To win thy will with mine for to consent,
Maintains that vow which love in me first wrought,
I love thee still, and never shall repent,
That happy hand which hardly did touch
Thy tender body to my deep delight,
Shall serve with sword to prove my passion such
As loves thee still, much more than it can write.
    Thus love I still with tongue, hand, heart and all,
      And when I change, let vengeance on me fall.

GEORGE GASCOIGNE (*c.* 1525—1577)

HE FUMBLES AT YOUR SPIRIT

He fumbles at your spirit
    As players at the keys
Before they drop full music on;
    He stuns you by degrees,

Prepares your brittle substance
    For the ethereal blow,
By fainter hammers, further heard,
    Then nearer, then so slow

Your breath has time to straighten,
    Your brain to bubble cool, –
Deals one imperial thunderbolt
    That scalps your naked soul.

SYRINX

Pan's Syrinx was a girl indeed,
Though now she's turned into a reed;
From that dear reed Pan's pipe does come,
A pipe that strikes Apollo dumb;
Nor flute, nor lute, nor gittern can
So chant it as the pipe of Pan:
Cross-gartered swains and dairy girls,
With faces smug and round as pearls,
When Pan's shrill pipe begins to play,
With dancing wear out night and day:
The bagpipe's drone his hum lays by
When Pan sounds up his minstrelsy;
His minstrelsy! oh, base! this quill –
Which at my mouth with wind I fill –
Puts me in mind, though her I miss,
That still my Syrinx' lips I kiss.

JOHN LYLY (?1554–1606)

LOVE

Love is a sickness full of woes,
   All remedies refusing;
A plant that with most cutting grows,
   Most barren with best using.
         Why so?
More we enjoy it, more it dies;
If not enjoyed, it sighing cries,
         Heigh ho!

Love is a torment of the mind,
   A tempest everlasting;
And Jove hath made it of a kind
   Not well, nor full, nor fasting.
         Why so?
More we enjoy it, more it dies;
If not enjoyed, it sighing cries,
         Heigh ho!

IF THE DULL SUBSTANCE OF MY FLESH WERE THOUGHT

If the dull substance of my flesh were thought,
Injurious distance should not stop my way;
For then, despite of space, I would be brought,
From limits far remote, where thou dost stay.
No matter then although my foot did stand
Upon the farthest earth removed from thee;
For nimble thought can jump both sea and land,
As soon as think the place where he would be,
But, ah, thought kills me, that I am not thought,
To leap large lengths of miles when thou art gone,
But that, so much of earth and water wrought,
I must attend time's leisure with my moan;
    Receiving naught by elements so slow
    But heavy tears, badges of either's woe.

WILLIAM SHAKESPEARE (1564–1616)

LATE AIR

From a magician's midnight sleeve
    the radio-singers
distribute all their love-songs
over the dew-wet lawns.
    And like a fortune-teller's
their marrow-piercing guesses are whatever you
    believe.

But on the Navy Yard aerial I find
    better witnesses
for love on summer nights.
Five remote red lights
    keep their nests there; Phoenixes
burning quietly, where the dew cannot climb.

THE GOLDFINCH

My goldfinch, I'll throw back my head,
let's look at the world together:
the winter's day is prickly like chaff,
does it seem as harsh to your eyes?

Do you realise, goldfinch,
what a flash finch you are, with your little tail-feathers
like a rowboat, feathers – black and yellow,
your throat, flowing with colour.

What airy thoughts does he have in his mind?
He looks back and forth, he's on guard.
Now he's not looking, he's flown off,
a flash of black and red, yellow and white!

OSIP MANDELSTAM (1891–?1938)   159
TRANS. RICHARD AND ELIZABETH McKANE

THE WINDHOVER
To Christ our Lord

I caught this morning morning's minion, king-
   dom of daylight's dauphin, dapple-dawn-drawn
     Falcon, in his riding
   Of the rolling level underneath him steady air,
     and striding
High there, how he rung upon the rein of a wimpling wing
In his ecstasy! then off, off forth on swing,
   As a skate's heel sweeps smooth on a bow-bend:
     the hurl and gliding
   Rebuffed the big wind. My heart in hiding
Stirred for a bird, – the achieve of, the mastery
     of the thing!

Brute beauty and valour and act, oh, air, pride, plume, here
   Buckle! AND the fire that breaks from thee then, a billion
Times told lovelier, more dangerous, O my chevalier!

   No wonder of it: shéer plód makes plough down
     sillion
Shine, and blue-bleak embers, ah my dear,
   Fall, gall themselves, and gash gold-vermilion.

I FIND NO PEACE, AND ALL
MY WAR IS DONE

I find no peace, and all my war is done,
I fear, and hope. I burn, and freeze like ice.
I fly above the wind, yet can I not arise.
And naught I have, and all the world I season.
That loseth nor locketh holdeth me in prison,
And holdeth me not, yet can I 'scape nowise:
Nor letteth me live nor die at my devise,
And yet of death it giveth me occasion.
Without eyen I see, and without tongue I 'plain;
I desire to perish, and yet I ask health;
I love another, and thus I hate myself;
I feed me in sorrow, and laugh at all my pain.
    Likewise displeaseth me both death and life,
      And my delight is causer of this strife.

SIR THOMAS WYATT (1503–1542)

COME SLEEP, O SLEEP!

Come Sleep, O Sleep! the certain knot of peace,
    The baiting-place of wit, the balm of woe,
The poor man's wealth, the prisoner's release,
    The indifferent judge between the high and low;
With shield of proof shield me from out the prease
    Of those fierce darts Despair at me doth throw:
Oh, make in me those civil wars to cease!
    I will good tribute pay if thou do so.
Take thou of me smooth pillows, sweetest bed,
    A chamber deaf to noise and blind of light,
A rosy garland and a weary head:
    And if these things, as being thine by right,
        Move not thy heavy grace, thou shalt in me
        Livelier than elsewhere Stella's image see.

IF THERE WERE ...

The author loving these homely meats specially, viz.: cream,
pancakes, buttered pippin-pies (laugh, good people) and
tobacco; writ to that worthy and virtuous gentlewoman,
whom he calleth mistress, as followeth

> If there were, oh! an Hellespont of cream
> Between us, milk-white mistress, I would swim
> To you, to show to both my love's extreme,
> Leander-like, – yea! dive from brim to brim.
> But met I with a buttered pippin-pie
> Floating upon 't, that would I make my boat
> To waft me to you without jeopardy,
> Though sea-sick I might be while it did float.
> Yet if a storm should rise, by night or day,
> Of sugar-snows and hail of caraways,
> Then, if I found a pancake in my way,
> It like a plank should bring me to your kays;
> > Which having found, if they tobacco kept,
> > The smoke should dry me well before I slept.

IF MUSIC AND SWEET POETRY
AGREE

If Music and sweet Poetry agree,
As they must needs, (the sister and the brother),
Then must the love be great 'twixt thee and me,
Because thou lovest the one and I the other.
Dowland to thee is dear, whose heavenly touch
Upon the lute doth ravish human sense;
Spenser to me, whose deep conceit is such
As, passing all conceit, needs no defence.
Thou lovest to hear the sweet melodious sound
That Phoebus' lute, the Queen of Music, makes;
And I in deep delight am chiefly drowned
Whenas himself to singing he betakes.
One god is god of both, as poets feign;
One knight loves both, and both in thee remain.

AN DEM STILLEN MEERESSTRANDE

Night has come with silent footsteps,
  On the beaches by the ocean;
And the waves, with curious whispers,
  Ask the moon, 'Have you a notion

'Who that man is? Is he foolish,
  Or with love is he demented?
For he seems so sad and cheerful,
  So cast down yet so contented.'

And the moon, with shining laughter,
  Answers them, 'If you must know it,
He is both in love *and* foolish;
  And, besides that, he's a poet!'

HEINRICH HEINE (1797–1856)   165
TRANS. LOUIS UNTERMEYER

THE MAGNET

Ask the Empresse of the night
    How the hand which guides her sphear,
Constant in unconstant light,
    Taught the waves her yoke to bear,
And did thus by loving force
Curb or tame the rude seas course.

Ask the female Palme how shee
    First did woo her husbands love;
And the Magnet, ask how he
    Doth th' obsequious iron move;
Waters, plants and stones know this,
That they love, not what love is.

Be not then less kind than these,
    Or from love exempt alone,
Let us twine like amorous trees,
    And like rivers melt in one;
Or if thou more cruell prove
Learne of steel and stones to love.

SONG

The Lark now leaves his watry Nest
    And climbing, shakes his dewy Wings;
He takes this Window for the East;
    And to implore your Light, he Sings,
Awake, awake, the Morn will never rise,
Till she can dress her Beauty at your Eies.

The Merchant bowes unto the Seamans Star,
    The Ploughman from the Sun his Season takes;
But still the Lover wonders what they are,
    Who look for day before his Mistress wakes.
Awake, awake, break through your Vailes of Lawne!
Then draw your Curtains, and begin the Dawne.

SIR WILLIAM DAVENANT (1606–1668)

TRANSIT

A woman I have never seen before
Steps from the darkness of her town-house door
At just that crux of time when she is made
So beautiful that she or time must fade.

What use to claim that as she tugs her gloves
A phantom heraldry of all the loves
Blares from the lintel? That the staggered sun
Forgets, in his confusion, how to run?

Still, nothing changes as her perfect feet
Click down the walk that issues in the street,
Leaving the stations of her body there
As a whip maps the countries of the air.

SONNET: WHAT IS NEEDED

A complete new sex. Not those dreary old
    men and women,
where the beautiful are so pleased to be beautiful
and the unattractive live in outer darkness;
but a real democracy where everyone's
    equal and opposite
and nobody's under proof. Satisfaction guaranteed.
That would be something. If jealousy and frustration
could be thrown into the everlasting dustbin,
what an end to sourness and the moulds of madness!
We live, however, in an unregenerate country.
There's no sign yet of that desired mutation.
Monsters are wearing briefs and ties and waistcoats
and filling the world with hours of quiet agony.
Sprightliness wears the bowler hats of boredom
and young difficulties fill the bras and panties.

GAVIN EWART (1916–1996)   169

From MODERN LOVE

i

Am I failing? For no longer can I cast
A glory round about this head of gold.
Glory she wears, but springing from the mould;
Not like the consecration of the Past!
Is my soul beggared? Something more than earth
I cry for still: I cannot be at peace
In having Love upon a mortal lease.
I cannot take the woman at her worth!
Where is the ancient wealth wherewith I clothed
Our human nakedness, and could endow
With spiritual splendour a white brow
That else had grinned at me the fact I loathed?
A kiss is but a kiss now! and no wave
Of a great flood that whirls me to the sea.
But, as you will! we'll sit contentedly,
And eat our pot of honey on the grave.

ii

What are we first? First, animals; and next
Intelligences at a leap; on whom
Pale lies the distant shadow of the tomb,
And all that draweth on the tomb for text.
Into which state comes Love, the crowning sun:
Beneath whose light the shadow loses form.
We are the lords of life, and life is warm.
Intelligence and instinct now are one.
But nature says: 'My children most they seem
When they least know me: therefore I decree
That they shall suffer.' Swift doth young Love flee,
And we stand wakened, shivering from our dream.
Then if we study Nature we are wise.
Thus do the few who live but with the day:
The scientific animals are they. –
Lady, this is my sonnet to your eyes.

GEORGE MEREDITH (1828–1909)   171

SONNET: A DREAM

The feeling tone was one of lost love,
bitter, as I woke with a cigar mouth;
but, as Bing Crosby and others have said and
sung, it's better, etc. You can't lose love
unless at one time, in some way, you had it.
As one grows older, one grows reconciled.
The names of the lost are at home in other beds
with difficulties of their own. Not including me.

Dreams work with a kind of neat backslang.
Love could be evol; and the boy a yob.
The approved thing is to be in love with Efil,
she's the girl you ought to fancy. She
is the warm abstraction books call positive.
I like her; but you couldn't call it love.

MORE AND MORE

More and more frequently the edges
of me dissolve and I become
a wish to assimilate the world, including
you, if possible through the skin
like a cool plant's tricks with oxygen
and live by a harmless green burning.

I would not consume
you, or ever
finish, you would still be there
surrounding me, complete
as the air.

Unfortunately, I don't have leaves.
Instead I have eyes
and teeth and other non-green things
which rule out osmosis.

So be careful, I mean it,
I give you a fair warning:

This kind of hunger draws
everything into its own
space; nor can we
talk it over, have a calm
rational discussion.

There is no reason for this, only
a starved dog's logic about bones.

MARGARET ATWOOD (b. 1939)   173

LUCK

Sometimes a crumb falls
From the tables of joy,
Sometimes a bone
Is flung.

To some people
Love is given,
To others
Only heaven.

THE FROG PRINCE

I am a frog
I live under a spell
I live at the bottom
Of a green well

And here I must wait
Until a maiden places me
On her royal pillow
And kisses me
In her father's palace.

The story is familiar
Everybody knows it well
But do other enchanted people feel as nervous
As I do? The stories do not tell,

Ask if they will be happier
When the changes come
As already they are fairly happy
In a frog's doom?

I have been a frog now
For a hundred years
And in all this time
I have not shed many tears,

I am happy, I like the life,
Can swim for many a mile

(When I have hopped to the river)
And am for ever agile.

And the quietness,
Yes, I like to be quiet
I am habituated
To a quiet life,

But always when I think these thoughts
As I sit in my well
Another thought comes to me and says:
It is part of the spell

To be happy
To work up contentment
To make much of being a frog
To fear disenchantment

Says, It will be *heavenly*
To be set free,
Cries, *Heavenly* the girl who disenchants
And the royal times, *heavenly*,
And I think it will be.

Come then, royal girl and royal times,
Come quickly,
I can be happy until you come
But I cannot be heavenly,
Only disenchanted people
Can be heavenly.

COAT

Sometimes I have wanted
to throw you off
like a heavy coat.

Sometimes I have said
you would not let me
breathe or move.

But now that I am free
to choose light clothes
or none at all

I feel the cold
and all the time I think
how warm it used to be.

HAPPY ENDING

After they had not made love
she pulled the sheet up over her eyes
until he was buttoning his shirt:
not shyness for their bodies – those
they had willingly displayed – but a frail
endeavour to apologise.

Later, though, drawn together by
a distaste for such 'untidy ends'
they agreed to meet again; whereupon
they giggled, reminisced, held hands
as though what they had made was love –
and not that happier outcome, friends.

PASTORAL DIALOGUE

Remember when you love, from that same hour
Your peace you put into your lover's power;
From that same hour from him you laws receive,
And as he shall ordain, you joy, or grieve,
Hope, fear, laugh, weep; Reason aloof does stand,
Disabled both to act, and to command.
Oh cruel fetters! rather wish to feel
On your soft limbs, the galling weight of steel;
Rather to bloody wounds oppose your breast.
No ill, by which the body can be pressed
You will so sensible a torment find
As shackles on your captivated mind.
The mind from heaven its high descent did draw,
And brooks uneasily any other law
Than what from Reason dictated shall be.
Reason, a kind of innate deity,
Which only can adapt to ev'ry soul
A yoke so fit and light, that the control
All liberty excells; so sweet a sway,
The same 'tis to be happy, and obey;
Commands so wise, and with rewards so dressed,
That the according soul replies 'I'm blessed'.

ANNE KILLIGREW (1660–1685)   179

BLANK JOY

She who did not come, wasn't she determined
nonetheless to organize and decorate my heart?
If we had to exist to become the one we love,
what would the heart have to create?

Lovely joy left blank, perhaps you are
the center of all my labors and my loves.
If I've wept for you so much, it's because
I preferred you among so many outlined joys.

RAINER MARIA RILKE (1875–1926)
TRANS. A. POULIN JR.

OF LOVE. A SONET

How Love came in, I do not know,
Whether by th' eye, or eare, or no:
Or whether with the soule it came
(At first) infused with the same:
Whether in part 'tis here or there,
Or, like the soule, whole every where:
This troubles me: but I as well
As any other, this can tell;
That when from hence she does depart,
The out-let then is from the heart.

ROBERT HERRICK (1591–1674)

DELIRIUM IN VERA CRUZ

Where has tenderness gone, he asked the mirror
Of the Biltmore Hotel, cuarto 216. Alas,
Can its reflection lean against the glass
Too, wondering where I have gone, into what horror?
Is that it staring at me now with terror
Behind your frail tilted barrier? Tenderness
Was here, in this very bedroom, in this
Place, its form seen, cries heard, by you. What error
Is here? Am I that rashed image?
Is this the ghost of the love you reflected?
Now with a background of tequila, stubs, dirty collars,
Sodium perborate, and a scrawled page
To the dead, telephone off the hook? In rage
He smashed all the glass in the room. (Bill: $50.)

TO HIS LOVE

He's gone, and all our plans
   Are useless indeed.
We'll walk no more on Cotswold
   Where the sheep feed
   Quietly and take no heed.

His body that was so quick
   Is not as you
Knew it, on Severn river
   Under the blue
   Driving our small boat through.

You would not know him now ...
   But still he died
Nobly, so cover him over
   With violets of pride
   Purple from Severn side.

Cover him, cover him soon!
   And with thick-set
Masses of memoried flowers –
   Hide that red wet
   Thing I must somehow forget.

IVOR GURNEY (1890–1937)

WANTS

Beyond all this, the wish to be alone:
However the sky grows dark with invitation-cards
However we follow the printed directions of sex
However the family is photographed under the
    flagstaff –
Beyond all this, the wish to be alone.

Beneath it all, desire of oblivion runs:
Despite the artful tensions of the calendar,
The life insurance, the tabled fertility rites,
The costly aversion of the eyes from death –
Beneath it all, desire of oblivion runs.

ALL MY GOODBYES ARE SAID

All my goodbyes are said. Many separations
slowly shaped me since my infancy.
But I come back again and I begin again;
this fresh return releases my attention.

What's left for me is to replenish it,
and my joy, forever unrepentant
for having loved the things resembling
these absences that make us act.

RAINER MARIA RILKE (1875–1926)   185
TRANS. A. POULIN JR.

WINDING UP

I live on the water,
alone. Without wife and children.
I have circled every possibility
to come to this:

a low house by grey water,
with windows always open
to the stale sea. We do not choose such things,

but we are what we have made.
We suffer, the years pass,
we shed freight but not our need

for encumbrances. Love is a stone
that settled on the seabed
under grey water. Now, I require nothing

from poetry but true feeling,
no pity, no fame, no healing. Silent wife,
we can sit watching grey water,

and in a life awash
with mediocrity and trash
live rock-like.

I shall unlearn feeling,
unlearn my gift. That is greater
and harder than what passes there for life.

IN TIME LIKE AIR

Consider the mysterious salt:
In water it must disappear.
It has no self. It knows no fault.
Not even sight may apprehend it.
No one may gather it or spend it.
It is dissolved and everywhere.

But, out of water into air,
It must resolve into a presence,
Precise and tangible and here.
Faultlessly pure, faultlessly white,
It crystallizes in our sight
And has defined itself to essence.

What element dissolves the soul
So it may be both found and lost,
In what suspended as a whole?
What is the element so blest
That there identity can rest
As salt in the clear water cast?

Love, in its early transformation,
And only love, may so design it
That the self flows in pure sensation,
Is all dissolved, and found at last
Without a future or a past,
And a whole life suspended in it.

The faultless crystal of detachment
Comes after, cannot be created
Without the first intense attachment.
Even the saints achieve this slowly;
For us, more human and less holy,
In time like air is essence stated.

LOVE AFTER LOVE

The time will come
when, with elation,
you will greet yourself arriving
at your own door, in your own mirror,
and each will smile at the other's welcome,

and say, sit here. Eat.
You will love again the stranger who was your self.
Give wine. Give bread. Give back your heart
to itself, to the stranger who has loved you

all your life, whom you ignored
for another, who knows you by heart.
Take down the love letters from the bookshelf,

the photographs, the desperate notes,
peel your own image from the mirror.
Sit. Feast on your life.

DEREK WALCOTT (b. 1930)   189

THE INFINITE

That hill pushed off by itself was always dear
to me and the hedges near
it that cut away so much of the final horizon.
When I would sit there lost in deliberation,
I reasoned most on the interminable spaces
beyond all hills,
the silence beyond my possibility.
Here for a little my heart is quiet inside me;
and when the wind lifts roughing through the trees,
I set about comparing my silence to those sounds,
I think about the infinite, the dead seasons,
this one that is present and alive,
the rumors we leave behind us, our small choice . . .
it is sweet to destroy my mind, and drown in this sea.

       AFTER GIACOMO LEOPARDI

HAPPY THE MAN

Happy the man who, journeying far and wide
As Jason or Ulysses did, can then
Turn homeward, seasoned in the ways of men,
And claim his own, and there in peace abide!

When shall I see the chimney-smoke divide
The sky above my little town: ah, when
Stroll the small gardens of that house again
Which is my realm and crown, and more beside?

Better I love the plain, secluded home
My fathers built, than bold façades of Rome;
Slate pleases me as marble cannot do;

Better than Tiber's flood my quiet Loire,
Those little hills than these, and dearer far
Than great sea winds the zephyrs of Anjou.

JOACHIM DU BELLAY (1522–1560)   191
TRANS. RICHARD WILBUR

STRANGERS

There have been two strangers
Who met within a wood
And looked once at each other
Where they stood.

And there have been two strangers
Who met among the heather
And did not look at all
But lay down together.

And there have been two strangers
Who met one April day
And looked long at each other,
And went their way.

O MY FRIENDS

O my friends, all of you, I renounce
none of you: not even that transient
who, from the inconceivable life, was
no more than a soft glance, open and hesitant.

How often, with an eye or gesture,
someone, despite himself, stops
the imperceptible flight of another
by paying attention to him a moment.

Strangers. They play large parts
in our fate that every day completes.
O discreet stranger, take good aim,
as you lift your gaze towards my distracted heart.

RAINER MARIA RILKE (1875—1926)
TRANS A. POULIN JR.

ONE ART

The art of losing isn't hard to master;
so many things seem filled with the intent
to be lost that their loss is no disaster.

Lose something every day. Accept the fluster
of lost door keys, the hour badly spent.
The art of losing isn't hard to master.

Then practice losing farther, losing faster:
places, and names, and where it was you meant
to travel. None of these will bring disaster.

I lost my mother's watch. And look! my last, or
next-to-last, of three loved houses went.
The art of losing isn't hard to master.

I lost two cities, lovely ones. And, vaster,
some realms I owned, two rivers, a continent.
I miss them, but it wasn't a disaster.

— Even losing you (the joking voice, a gesture
I love) I shan't have lied. It's evident
the art of losing's not too hard to master
though it may look like (*Write* it!) like disaster.

HOMECOMING

I went back in the alley
And I opened up my door.
All her clothes was gone:
She wasn't home no more.

I pulled back the covers,
I made down the bed.
A *whole* lot of room
Was the only thing I had.

A LIGHT LEFT ON

In the evening we came back
Into our yellow room,
For a moment taken aback
To find the light left on,
Falling on silent flowers,
Table, book, empty chair
While we had gone elsewhere,
Had been away for hours.

When we came home together
We found the inside weather.
All of our love unended
The quiet light demanded,
And we gave, in a look
At yellow walls and open book.
The deepest world we share
And do not talk about
But have to have, was there,
And by that light found out.

WITHOUT HER

What of her glass without her? the blank grey
   There where the pool is blind of the moon's face.
   Her dress without her? the tossed empty space
Of cloud-rack whence the moon has passed away.
Her paths without her? Day's appointed sway
   Usurped by desolate night. Her pillowed place
   Without her! Tears, Ah me! for love's good grace
And cold forgetfulness of night or day.
What of the heart without her? Nay, poor heart,
   Of thee what word remains ere speech be still?
   A wayfarer by barren ways and chill,
Steep ways and weary, without her thou art,
Where the long cloud, the long wood's counterpart,
   Sheds doubled darkness up the labouring hill.

THE APPARITION

My pillow won't tell me
    Where he has gone,
The soft-footed one
    Who passed by, alone.

Who took my heart, whole,
    With a tilt of his eye,
And with it, my soul,
    And it like to die.

I twist, and I turn,
    My breath but a sigh.
Dare I grieve? Dare I mourn?
    He walks by. He walks by.

FUNERAL BLUES

Stop all the clocks, cut off the telephone,
Prevent the dog from barking with a juicy bone,
Silence the pianos and with muffled drum
Bring out the coffin, let the mourners come.

Let aeroplanes circle moaning overhead
Scribbling on the sky the message He Is Dead,
Put crêpe bows round the white necks of
    the public doves,
Let the traffic policemen wear black cotton gloves.

He was my North, my South, my East and West,
My working week and my Sunday rest,
My noon, my midnight, my talk, my song;
I thought that love would last for ever: I was wrong.

The stars are not wanted now: put out every one;
Pack up the moon and dismantle the sun;
Pour away the ocean and sweep up the wood;
For nothing now can ever come to any good.

W. H. AUDEN (1907–1973) 199

PRAISE OF A COLLIE

She was a small dog, neat and fluid –
Even her conversation was tiny:
She greeted you with *bow*, never *bow-wow*.

Her sons stood monumentally over her
But did what she told them. Each grew grizzled
Till it seemed he was his own mother's grandfather.

Once, gathering sheep on a showery day,
I remarked how dry she was. Pollóchan said, 'Ah,
It would take a very accurate drop to hit Lassie.'

She sailed in the dinghy like a proper sea-dog.
Where's a burn? – she's first on the other side.
She flowed through fences like a piece of black wind.

But suddenly she was old and sick and crippled . . .
I grieved for Pollóchan when he took her a stroll
And put his gun to the back of her head.

ANGUS'S DOG

Black collie, do you remember yourself?

Do you remember your name was Mephistopheles,
though (as if you were only a little devil)
everyone called you Meph?

You'd chase everything – sea gulls, motor cars,
jet planes. (It's said you once set off
after a lightning flash.) Half over a rock,
you followed the salmon fly arcing
through the bronze water. You loved everything
except rabbits – though
you grinned away under the bed
when your master came home
drink taken. How you'd lay your head
on a visitor's knee and look up, so soulfully,
like George Eliot playing Sarah Bernhardt.

... Black Meph, how can you remember yourself
in that blank no-time, no-place where
you can't even greet your master
though he's there too?

NORMAN MacCAIG (1910–1996)   201

FOR A GOOD DOG

My little dog ten years ago
Was arrogant and spry,
Her backbone was a bended bow
For arrows in her eye.
Her step was proud, her bark was loud,
Her nose was in the sky,
But she was ten years younger then,
And so, by God, was I.

Small birds on stilts along the beach
Rose up with piping cry,
And as they flashed beyond her reach
I thought to see her fly.
If natural law refused her wings,
That law she would defy,
For she could do unheard-of things,
And so, at times, could I.

Ten years ago she split the air
To seize what she could spy;
Tonight she bumps against a chair,
Betrayed by milky eye.
She seems to pant, Time up, time up!
My little dog must die,
And lie in dust with Hector's pup;
So, presently, must I.

OGDEN NASH (1902–1971)

THE DOG

The truth I do not stretch or shove
When I state the dog is full of love.
I've also proved, by actual test,
A wet dog is the lovingest.

OGDEN NASH (1902–1971)

NODDING

Tizdal my beautiful cat
Lies on the old rag mat
In front of the kitchen fire.
Outside the night is black.

The great fat cat
Lies with his paws under him
His whiskers twitch in a dream,
He is slumbering.

The clock on the mantelpiece
Ticks unevenly, tic toc, tic-toc,
Good heavens what is the matter
With the kitchen clock?

Outside an owl hunts,
Hee hee hee hee,
Hunting in the Old Park
From his snowy tree.
What on earth can he find in the park tonight,
It is so wintry?

Now the fire burns suddenly too hot
Tizdal gets up to move,
Why should such an animal
Provoke our love?

The twigs from the elder bush
Are tapping on the window pane
As the wind sets them tapping,
Now the tapping begins again.

One laughs on a night like this
In a room half firelight half dark
With a great lump of a cat
Moving on the hearth,
And the twigs tapping quick,
And the owl in an absolute fit
One laughs supposing creation
Pays for its long plodding
Simply by coming to this –
Cat, night, fire – and a girl nodding.

STEVIE·SMITH (1902−1971)   205

BRISE MARINE

K with quick laughter, honey skin and hair,
and always money. In what beach shade, what year
has she so scented with her gentleness
I cannot watch bright water but think of her
and that fine morning when she sang O rare
Ben's lyric of 'the bag o' the bee'
and 'the nard in the fire'
                'nard in the fire'
against the salty music of the sea
the fresh breeze tangling each honey tress
              and what year was the fire?
Girls' faces dim with time Andreuille all gold ...
Sunday. The grass peeps through the breaking pier.
Tables in the trees, like entering Renoir.
Maintenant je n'ai plus ni fortune, ni pouvoir ...
But when the light was setting through thin hair,
Holding whose hand by what trees, what old wall.

Two honest women, Christ, where are they gone?
Out of that wonder, what do I recall?
The darkness closing round a fisherman's oar.
The sound of water gnawing at bright stone.

TO PRAISE A DEAD WOMAN

Is it possible to praise a dead woman?
She is estranged and powerful . . .
An alien-loving power has brought her
to a violent, hot grave.

The rigid swallows of her curved brows
flew to me from the grave
to say they had laid down to rest
in their cold Stockholm bed.

Your family were proud of your
        great-grandfather's violin,
and it was beautiful at the neck.
You parted your scarlet lips
in laughter, so Italian, so Russian.

I cherish your unhappy memory,
wilding, bear cub, Mignon.
But the wheels of the windmills hibernate in the snow,
and the postman's horn is frozen.

OSIP MANDELSTAM (1891–?1938)   207
TRANS. RICHARD AND ELIZABETH McKANE

LOVE

Two thousand cigarettes.
A hundred miles
from wall to wall.
An eternity and a half of vigils
blanker than snow.

Tons of words
old as the tracks
of a platypus in the sand.

A hundred books we didn't write.
A hundred pyramids we didn't build.

Sweepings.
Dust.

Bitter
as the beginning of the world.

Believe me when I say
it was beautiful.

208   MIROSLAV HOLUB (b. 1923)
      TRANS. IAN MILNER

UPON HIS LEAVING HIS MISTRESS

'Tis not that I am weary grown
Of being yours, and yours alone;
But with what face can I incline
To damn you to be only mine?
   You, whom some kinder power did fashion,
   By merit and by inclination,
   The joy at least of one whole nation.

Let meaner spirits of your sex
With humbler aims their thoughts perplex,
And boast if by their arts they can
Contrive to make *one* happy man;
   Whilst, moved by an impartial sense,
   Favours like nature you dispense
   With universal influence.

See, the kind seed-receiving earth
To every grain affords a birth.
On her no showers unwelcome fall;
Her willing womb retains 'em all.
   And shall my Celia be confined?
   No! Live up to thy mighty mind,
   And be the mistress of mankind.

ENDING

The love we thought would never stop
now cools like a congealing chop.
The kisses that were hot as curry
are bird-pecks taken in a hurry.
The hands that held electric charges
now lie inert as four moored barges.
The feet that ran to meet a date
are running slow and running late.
The eyes that shone and seldom shut
are victims of a power cut.
The parts that then transmitted joy
are now reserved and cold and coy.
Romance, expected once to stay,
has left a note saying GONE AWAY.

COOTCHIE

Cootchie, Miss Lula's servant, lies in marl,
black into white she went
    below the surface of the coral-reef.
Her life was spent
    in caring for Miss Lula, who is deaf,
eating her dinner off the kitchen sink
while Lula ate hers off the kitchen table.
The skies were egg-white for the funeral
    and the faces sable.

Tonight the moonlight will alleviate
the melting of the pink wax roses
    planted in tin cans filled with sand
placed in a line to mark Miss Lula's losses;
    but who will shout and make her understand?
Searching the land and sea for someone else,
the lighthouse will discover Cootchie's grave
and dismiss all as trivial; the sea, desperate.
    will proffer wave after wave.

ELIZABETH BISHOP (1911–1979) 211

TO HIS DYING BROTHER, MASTER WILLIAM HERRICK

Life of my life, take not so soone thy flight,
But stay the time till we have bade Good night.
Thou hast both Wind and Tide with thee; Thy way
As soone dispatcht is by the Night, as Day.
Let us not then so rudely henceforth goe
Till we have wept, kist, sigh't, shook hands, or so.
There's paine in parting; and a kind of hell,
When once true-lovers take their last Fare-well.
What? shall we two our endlesse leaves take here
Without a sad looke, or a solemne teare?
He knowes not Love, that hath not this truth proved,
Love is most loth to leave the thing beloved.
Pay we our Vowes, and goe; yet when we part,
Then, even then, I will bequeath my heart
Into thy loving hands: For Ile keep none
To warme my Breast, when thou my Pulse art gone.
No, here Ile last, and walk (a harmless shade)
About this Urne, wherein thy Dust is laid,
To guard it so, as nothing here shall be
Heavy, to hurt those sacred seeds of thee.

WITH HER

Those poor, arthritically swollen knees
Of my mother in an absent country.
I think of them on my seventy-fourth birthday
As I attend early Mass at St. Mary Magdalen
     in Berkeley.
A reading this Sunday from the Book of Wisdom
About how God has not made death
And does not rejoice in the annihilation of the living.
A reading from the Gospel according to Mark
About a little girl to whom He said: 'Talitha, cumi!'
This is for me. To make me rise from the dead
And repeat the hope of those who lived before me,
In a fearful unity with her, with her pain of dying,
In a village near Danzig, in a dark November,
When both the mournful Germans, old men and
     women,
And the evacuees from Lithuania would fall ill
     with typhus.
Be with me, I say to her, my time has been short.
Your words are now mine, deep inside me:
'It all seems now to have been a dream.'

CZESLAW MILOSZ (b. 1911)   213

CHILDREN OF DARKNESS

We spurred our parents to the kiss,
Though doubtfully they shrank from this –
Day had no courage to pursue
What lusty dark alone might do:
Then were we joined from their caress
In heat of midnight, one from two.

This night-seed knew no discontent:
In certitude our changings went.
Though there were veils about his face,
With forethought, even in that pent place,
Down toward the light his way we bent
To kingdoms of more ample space.

Is Day prime error, that regret
For Darkness roars unstifled yet?
That in this freedom, by faith won,
Only acts of doubt are done?
That unveiled eyes with tears are wet:
We loathe to gaze upon the sun?

MOTHER, 1972

More than once taking both roads one night
to shake the inescapable hold of New York –
now more than before fearing everything I do
is only (only) a mix of mother and father,
no matter how unlike they were, they are –
it's not what you were or thought, but you . . .
the choked oblique joke, the weighty luxurious stretch.
Mother, we are our true selves in the bath –
a cold splash each morning, the long hot evening loll.
O dying of your cerebral hemorrhage,
lost at Rapallo, dabbing your brow a week,
bruised from stumbling to your unceasing baths,
as if you hoped to drown your killer wound –
to keep me safe a generation after your death.

ROBERT LOWELL (1917–1977)   215

LONG DISTANCE 2

Though my mother was already two years dead
Dad kept her slippers warming by the gas,
put hot water bottles her side of the bed
and still went to renew her transport pass.

You couldn't just drop in. You had to phone.
He'd put you off an hour to give him time
to clear away her things and look alone
as though his still raw love were such a crime.

He couldn't risk my blight of disbelief
though sure that very soon he'd hear her key
scrape in the rusted lock and end his grief.
He *knew* she'd just popped out to get the tea.

I believe life ends with death, and that is all.
You haven't both gone shopping; just the same,
in my new black leather phone book there's your name
and the disconnected number I still call.

MOTHER, SUMMER, I

My mother, who hates thunderstorms,
Holds up each summer day and shakes
It out suspiciously, lest swarms
Of grape-dark clouds are lurking there;
But when the August weather breaks
And rains begin, and brittle frost
Sharpens the bird-abandoned air,
Her worried summer look is lost.

And I her son, though summer-born
And summer-loving, none the less
Am easier when the leaves are gone;
Too often summer days appear
Emblems of perfect happiness
I can't confront: I must await
A time less bold, less rich, less clear:
An autumn more appropriate.

PHILIP LARKIN (1922–1985)   217

CADET-PICTURE OF RILKE'S FATHER

There's absence in the eyes. The brow's in touch
with something far, and his enormous mouth,
tempted, serious, is a boy's unsmiling . . .
modest, counting on future promotion, stiff
in his slender aristocratic uniform –
both hands bulge on the basket-hilt of his saber.
They are quiet and reach out to nothing.
I can hardly see them now, as if
they were the first to grasp distance and disappear.
All the rest is curtained in itself,
and so faded I cannot understand
my father as he bleaches on this page –
You quickly disappearing daguerreotype
in my more slowly disappearing hand.

AFTER RAINER MARIA RILKE

FATHER'S INCANTATIONS

O sweet master, with how much peace
Your serene wisdom fills the heart!
I love you, I am in your power
Even though I will never see your face.

Your ashes have long been scattered,
Your sins and follies no one remembers.
And for ages you will remain perfect
Like your book drawn by thought from
        nothingness.

You knew bitterness and you knew doubt
But the memory of your faults has vanished.
And I know why I cherish you today:
Men are small but their works are great.

FOR AUNT SARAH

You never had the constitution to quarrel:
poised, warm and cool, distrusting hair and Hamlets,
yet infinitely kind – in short a lady,
still reaching for the turn of the century,
your youth in the solid golden age, when means
needed only to follow the golden mean
to love and care for the world; when businessmen
and their ancillary statesmen willingly gave up
health, wealth and pleasure for the gall of office –
converts to their only fiction, God.
But this new age? 'They have no fun,' you say . . .
We've quarreled lightly almost fifty years,
Dear, long enough to know how high our pulse beats,
     while the young
wish to stand in our shoes before we've left them.

BORN YESTERDAY
for Sally Amis

Tightly-folded bud,
I have wished you something
None of the others would:
Not the usual stuff
About being beautiful,
Or running off a spring
Of innocence and love –
They will all wish you that,
And should it prove possible,
Well, you're a lucky girl.

But if it shouldn't, then
May you be ordinary;
Have, like other women,
An average of talents:
Not ugly, not good-looking,
Nothing uncustomary
To pull you off your balance,
That, unworkable itself,
Stops all the rest from working.
In fact, may you be dull –
If that is what a skilled,
Vigilant, flexible,
Unemphasised, enthralled
Catching of happiness is called.

PHILIP LARKIN (1922–1985)   221

LETTY'S GLOBE

When Letty had scarce passed her third glad year,
And her young artless words began to flow,
One day we gave the child a coloured sphere
Of the wide earth, that she might mark and know,
By tint and outline, all its sea and land.
She patted all the world; old empires peeped
Between her baby fingers. Her soft hand
Was welcome at all frontiers. How she leaped,
And laughed, and prattled, in her world-wide bliss.
But when we turned her sweet unlearned eye
On our own isle, she raised a joyous cry,
'Oh! yes, I see it. Letty's home is there!'
And while she hid all England with a kiss,
Bright over Europe fell her golden hair.

TO MY MOTHER

Most near, most dear, most loved and most far,
Under the window where I often found her
Sitting as huge as Asia, seismic with laughter,
Gin and chicken helpless in her Irish hand,
Irresistible as Rabelais, but most tender for
The lame dogs and hurt birds that surround her, –
She is a procession no one can follow after
But be like a little dog following a brass band.

She will not glance up at the bomber, or condescend
To drop her gin and scuttle to a cellar,
But lean on the mahogany table like a mountain
Whom only faith can move, and so I send
O all my faith, and all my love to tell her
That she will move from mourning into morning.

GEORGE BARKER (1913–1991)   223

MY PAPA'S WALTZ

The whiskey on your breath
Could make a small boy dizzy;
But I hung on like death:
Such waltzing was not easy.

We romped until the pans
Slid from the kitchen shelf;
My mother's countenance
Could not unfrown itself.

The hand that held my wrist
Was battered on one knuckle;
At every step you missed
My right ear scraped a buckle.

You beat time on my head
With a palm caked hard by dirt,
Then waltzed me off to bed
Still clinging to your shirt.

FROM FATHER TO SON

Reject the complicated life.
Look at your hand near the bread on the table:
how clear those two things on the clear cloth are
from father to son and from son to father.

Love the earth's celestial countryside
and its joy, hidden by manifest pain,
the quiet window, the harsh door
from father to son and from son to father.

And those kneeling things always in place
and the dog who fidgets, yet outdoes them,
very gentle believer who hardly doubts
from father to son and from son to father.

RAINER MARIA RILKE (1875–1926)
TRANS. A. POULIN JR.

THE ROAD

There where you see a green valley
And a road half-covered with grass,
Through an oak wood beginning to bloom
Children are returning home from school.

In a pencil case that opens sideways
Crayons rattle among crumbs of a roll
And a copper penny saved by every child
To greet the first spring cuckoo.

Sister's beret and brother's cap
Bob in the bushy underbrush,
A screeching jay hops in the branches
And long clouds float over the trees.

A red roof is already visible at the bend.
In front of the house father, leaning on a hoe,
Bows down, touches the unfolded leaves,
And from his flower bed inspects the
     whole region.

TENDER ONLY TO ONE

Tender only to one
Tender and true
The petals swing
To my fingering
Is it you, or you, or you?

Tender only to one
I do not know his name
And the friends who fall
To the petals' call
May think my love to blame.

Tender only to one
This petal holds a clue
The face it shows
But too well knows
Who I am tender to.

Tender only to one,
Last petal's latest breath
Cries out aloud
From the icy shroud
His name, his name is Death.

STEVIE SMITH (1902–1971)   227

MARIA WENTWORTH

Thomae *Comitis* Cleveland, *filia praemortua prima*
Virgineam animam exhalavit

An. Dom. 1632. Æt. suae 18

And here the precious dust is layd;
Whose purely temper'd Clay was made
So fine, that it the guest betray'd.

Else the soule grew so fast within,
It broke the outward shell of sinne,
And so was hatch'd a Cherubin.

In height, it soar'd to God above;
In depth, it did to knowledge move,
And spread in breadth to generall love.

Before, a pious duty shind
To Parents, courtesie behind,
On either side an equall mind,

Good to the Poore, to kindred deare,
To servants kind, to friendship cleare,
To nothing but her selfe, severe.

So though a Virgin, yet a Bride
To every Grace, she justifi'd
A chaste Poligamie, and dy'd.

Learne from hence (Reader) what small trust
We owe this world, where vertue must
Fraile as our flesh, crumble to dust.

ON PARTING WITH MY WIFE, JANINA

Women mourners were giving their sister to fire.
And fire, the same as we looked at together,
She and I, in marriage through long years,
Bound by an oath for good or ill, fire
In fireplaces in winter, campfires, fires of burning
    cities,
Elemental, pure, from the beginnings of the Earth,
Was taking away her streaming hair, gray,
Seized her lips and her neck, engulfed her, fire
That in human languages designates love.
I thought nothing of languages. Or of words of prayer.

I loved her, without knowing who she really was.
I inflicted pain on her, chasing my illusion.
I betrayed her with women, though faithful to her only.
We lived through much happiness and unhappiness,
Separations, miraculous rescues. And now, this ash.
And the sea battering the shore when I walk the empty
    boulevard.
And the sea battering the shore. And ordinary sorrow.

How to resist nothingness? What power
Preserves what once was, if memory does not last?
For I remember little. I remember so very little.
Indeed, moments restored would mean the
    Last Judgment
That is adjourned from day to day, by Mercy perhaps.

Fire, liberation from gravity. An apple does not fall,
A mountain moves from its place. Beyond the
    fire-curtain,
A lamb stands in the meadow of indestructible forms.
The souls in Purgatory burn. Heraclitus, crazy,
Sees the flame consuming the foundations of the world.
Do I believe in the Resurrection of the Flesh?
    Not of this ash.
I call, I beseech: elements, dissolve yourselves!
Rise into the other, let it come, kingdom!
Beyond the earthly fire compose yourselves anew!

MY DEAREST DUST

Epitaph on monument erected in 1641 by
Lady Catherine Dyer to her husband Sir William
Dyer in Colmworth Church, Bedfordshire

My dearest dust, could not thy hasty day
Afford thy drowzy patience leave to stay
One hower longer: so that we might either
Sate up, or gone to bedd together?
But since thy finisht labor hath possest
Thy weary limbs with early rest,
Enjoy it sweetly: and thy widdowe bride
Shall soone repose her by thy slumbering side.
Whose business, now, is only to prepare
My nightly dress, and call to prayre:
Mine eyes wax heavy and ye day growes old.
The dew falls thick, my beloved growes cold.
Draw, draw ye closed curtaynes: and make room:
My dear, my dearest dust; I come, I come.

SHE

I think the dead are tender. Shall we kiss? –
My lady laughs, delighting in what is.
If she but sighs, a bird puts out its tongue.
She makes space lonely with a lovely song.
She lilts a low soft language, and I hear
Down long sea-chambers of the inner ear.

We sing together; we sing mouth to mouth.
The garden is a river flowing south.
She cries out loud the soul's own secret joy;
She dances, and the ground bears her away.
She knows the speech of light, and makes it plain
A lively thing can come to life again.

I feel her presence in the common day,
In that slow dark that widens every eye.
She moves as water moves, and comes to me,
Stayed by what was, and pulled by what would be.

THEODORE ROETHKE (1908–1963)   233

COMMENT

Oh, life is a glorious cycle of song,
A medley of extemporanea;
And love is a thing that can never go wrong;
And I am Marie of Rumania.

ADVICE

Folks, I'm telling you,
birthing is hard
and dying is mean –
so get yourself
a little loving
in between.

ACKNOWLEDGMENTS

Thanks are due to the following copyright holders for permission to reprint:

ADCOCK, FLEUR: 'Happy Ending' from Fleur Adcock's *Selected Poems* (1979) reprinted by permission of Oxford University Press. APOLLINAIRE, GUILLAUME: 'The Ninth Secret Poem' is taken from Apollinaire: *Selected Poems* translated by Oliver Bernard, published by Anvil Press Poetry in 1986. ATWOOD, MARGARET: 'More and More' from *Poems 1965–75* published by Virago by permission of Little, Brown. AUDEN, W. H.: 'Funeral Blues', 'This Lunar Beauty' and 'Dear, though the night is gone' from *Collected Poems* by W. H. Auden published by Faber and Faber Ltd. 'Funeral Blues', 'This Lunar Beauty' and 'Dear, though the night is gone' from *W. H. Auden: Collected Poems* by W. H. Auden, edited by Edward Mendelson. Copyright © 1976 by Edward Mendelson, William Meredith and Monroe K. Spears, Executors of the Estate of W. H. Auden. Reprinted by permission of Random House Inc. BARKER, GEORGE: 'To My Mother' from *Collected Poems* by George Barker published by Faber and Faber Ltd. BELLOC, HILAIRE: 'Fatigue' from *Complete Verse* by permission of the Peters Fraser & Dunlop Group Ltd. BETJEMAN, JOHN: 'In a Bath Teashop' from *Collected Poems* by permission of John

237

238

Starred Coverlet', 'Children of Darkness' from *Collected Poems* published by Cassell, 1975. Reprinted by permission of Carcanet Press Limited. GURNEY, IVOR: 'To His Love', 'Silver Birch', 'The Love Song' from *Collected Poems of Ivor Gurney* edited by P. J. Kavanagh (1982), reprinted by permission of Oxford University Press. HEINE, HEINRICH: 'Mit deinen blauen Augen', 'Im wunderschönen Monat Mai', 'Es stehen unbeweglich', 'Sie liebten sich beide, doch keiner', 'Du bist wie eine Blume', translated by Aaron Kramer, from *Poems* published by Citadel Press. By permission of the Carol Publishing Group. Excerpts from *Heinrich Heine: Paradox and Poet, The Poems* by Louis Untermeyer, copyright 1937 by Harcourt Brace & Company and renewed 1965 by Louis Untermeyer, reprinted by permission of the publisher. HOLUB, MIROSLAV: 'Love' by Miroslav Holub, translated by Ian & Jarmila Milner, by kind permission of Bloodaxe Books. Taken from *Poems Before & After* by Miroslav Holub (Bloodaxe Books, 1990). HUGHES, LANGSTON: 'Homecoming', 'Luck', 'Juke Box' and 'Advice' from *Collected Poems* by Langston Hughes. Copyright © 1994 by the Estate of Langston Hughes. Reprinted by permission of Alfred A. Knopf Inc. 'Advice' reprinted by permission of Harold Ober Associates Inc. Copyright 1994 by the Estate of Langston Hughes. JENNINGS, ELIZABETH: 'One Flesh' from *Celebrations* by permission of David Higham

Chatto & Windus. MANDELSTAM, OSIP: 'To Praise a Dead
Woman', 'Black Candle', 'The Goldfinch' by Osip
Mandelstam, translated by Richard and Elizabeth
McKane, by kind permission of Bloodaxe Books. Taken
from *The Voronezh Notebooks* by Osip Mandelstam
(Bloodaxe Books, 1996). MILOSZ, CZESLAW: 'With Her',
'The Road', 'On Parting with My Wife, Janina',
'Father's Incantation' from *Collected Poems* by Czeslaw
Milosz © 1990 by Czeslaw Milosz, published by The
Ecco Press, reprinted by permission of The Ecco Press.
'With Her', 'The Road', 'On Parting with My Wife,
Janina', 'Father's Incantation' from *Czeslaw Milosz: The
Collected Poems 1931–1987* (Viking, 1988) copyright ©
Czeslaw Milosz Royalties, Inc., 1945, 1985, 1988. NASH,
OGDEN: 'For a Good Dog', 'To My Valentine', 'The
Cuckoo', 'Love under the Republicans (or Democrats)',
'The Purist', 'The Dog', from *Candy is Dandy* by
permission of André Deutsch Ltd. and by permission of
Curtis Brown Ltd. Copyright © 1970 by Ogden Nash,
renewed. PARKER, DOROTHY: 'Unfortunate Coincidence',
'Social Note', 'Symphony Recital', 'Comment' from *The
Portable Dorothy Parker* by Dorothy Parker copyright
1928, renewed © 1956 by Dorothy Parker, used by
permission of Viking Penguin, a division of Penguin
Books USA Inc. and Gerald Duckworth & Co. Ltd.
PORTER, PETER: 'His and Hers' from *Peter Porter's
Collected Poems* (1983) reprinted by permission of

244

INDEX OF FIRST LINES